# THE BEGINNERS PLANT-POWERED DIET GUIDE & COOKBOOK

EASY AND DELICIOUS RECIPES FOR A HEALTHY, PLANT-BASED LIFESTYLE

ALAN E. WALKER

Copyright © 2024 by Alan E. Walker

All rights reserved.

No part of this book may be reproduced in any form or by any electronic or mechanical means, including information storage and retrieval systems, without written permission from the author, except for the use of brief quotations in a book review.

The information in this book is provided for educational and informational purposes only. While the author and publisher have made every effort to ensure the accuracy and reliability of the information provided, they do not assume any responsibility for errors, omissions, or contrary interpretations of the subject matter herein. The reader is advised to verify any information they choose to rely on independently.

# CONTENTS

Introduction — v

**CHAPTER 1** — 1
Understanding a Plant-Based Diet — 1

**CHAPTER 2** — 13
Nutritional Needs for a Plant-Based Diet — 13

**CHAPTER 3** — 25
Setting Up Your Plant-Based Kitchen — 25

**CHAPTER 4** — 36
The ABCs of Plant-Based Cooking — 36

**CHAPTER 5** — 47
Rise and Shine: Plant-Based Breakfasts to Kick Start Your Day — 47

**CHAPTER 6** — 60
Midday Marvels: Plant-Based Lunches for Energy and Satisfaction — 60

**CHAPTER 7** — 74
Deliciously Satisfying: Plant-Based Dinners to Wrap Up Your Day — 74

**CHAPTER 8** — 87
Nourishing Bites: Plant-Based Snacks and Sides — 87

**CHAPTER 9** — 100
A Culinary World Tour: Global Flavors, Plant-Based Style — 100

**CHAPTER 10** — 114
Sweet Endings: Plant-Based Desserts and Baked Goods — 114

CHAPTER 11 127
Blend It Up: Plant-Based Beverages and
Smoothies 127

CHAPTER 12 139
Making Over Your Favorites: Plant-Based Style 139

Epilogue 156

References 159

# INTRODUCTION

Step into the vibrant, health-filled world of plant-based eating. The power of a plant-based diet is undeniable, and a wealth of research continually backs it up. It's a lifestyle that promotes overall well-being and fuels your body with the nutrients it craves. In embracing a plant-based diet, you're choosing a path of vitality, longevity, and a deepened respect for the planet.

But why choose "The Beginners Plant-Powered Diet Guide & Cookbook" as your companion on this journey? One word - simplicity. This book is designed to make your transition to a plant-based diet as simple as possible. It's packed with easy-to-follow recipes, practical tips, and clear, concise advice. It's your ticket to the world of plant-based eating, minus the confusion and the overwhelming jargon.

Navigating the plant-based landscape can be a daunting task, especially for beginners. There's so much information out there - some of it contradictory - making it difficult to

INTRODUCTION

know where to start. That's where this cookbook comes in. It's your guiding light, your roadmap to the plant-based world. It's designed to demystify the process, breaking it down into digestible nuggets of information and actionable steps.

Your journey begins here, in these pages. This book isn't just about recipes; it's about empowering you to make sustainable changes. It's about equipping you with the knowledge and skills to embrace a plant-based lifestyle confidently. It's about guiding you to better health and well-being.

And who am I to steer you on this journey? I am one who has walked this path, navigated the challenges, and reaped the immense rewards of a plant-based lifestyle. And now, I am committed to sharing this knowledge and passion with you.

This is not just a cookbook. It's a guide, a friend, a tool to inspire and facilitate your transition to a healthier, plant-based life. Welcome aboard this exciting journey to health and vitality. Let's explore the power of plant-based eating together.

# CHAPTER 1

## UNDERSTANDING A PLANT-BASED DIET

We are all too familiar with the saying, "You are what you eat," but have we ever considered its gravity? Quite literally, the foods we choose to eat are transformed into the cells, tissues, and energy that define us. So, let's pay homage to the foods that form the backbone of a plant-based diet: fruits and vegetables, whole grains, legumes, nuts and seeds, and plant-based proteins.

### F<small>RUITS AND</small> V<small>EGETABLES</small>: N<small>ATURE'S</small> C<small>ANDY</small>

No plant-based diet is complete without an abundance of fruits and vegetables. These brightly colored gems are teeming with vital nutrients like vitamins, minerals, fiber, and antioxidants that support a healthy body. From crisp apples to leafy greens, juicy oranges to earthy beets, each fruit and vegetable brings its unique nutritional profile to the table. And just like an artist uses a palette of colors to create a masterpiece, you'll use a variety of fruits and vegetables to create nourishing, delicious, and visually appealing meals.

Think about the last time you bit into a ripe, juicy peach. The burst of sweetness, the slightly tart aftertaste, and the juice dribbling down your chin - that's the power of fruits and vegetables. They're not only good for your health; they're a sensory delight.

### Whole Grains: Power-Packed Packages

Whole grains are the unsung heroes of a plant-based diet. These tiny powerhouses are packed with complex carbohydrates, fiber, vitamins, and minerals. Unlike their refined counterparts, whole grains retain all parts of the grain — the bran, germ, and endosperm. Foods like brown rice, oatmeal, quinoa, and whole-grain bread are excellent sources of whole grains.

Imagine cooking up a pot of nutty quinoa, its delicate grains fluffing up as they cook. Or the smell of freshly baked whole grain bread wafting through your kitchen. These are the simple pleasures that whole grains bring to a plant-based diet.

### Legumes: The Protein-Rich Powerhouses

When it comes to plant-based proteins, legumes are a non-negotiable. Beans, lentils, chickpeas, and peas are protein-rich and packed with fiber, iron, and B vitamins. They're versatile, affordable, and can be used in countless ways.

Picture yourself preparing a hearty lentil soup on a cold winter day, the rich aroma filling your kitchen as the lentils simmer away. Or assembling a vibrant chickpea salad for a summer potluck, the colorful ingredients creating a feast for the eyes. That's the beauty of legumes - they're as nourishing as they are versatile.

### NUTS AND SEEDS: SMALL BUT MIGHTY

Nuts and seeds may be small, but they're mighty in their nutritional profile. Packed with heart-healthy fats, protein, fiber, and various vital minerals, nuts and seeds are integral to a plant-based diet. Each nut and seed, from almonds to chia seeds, brings a unique flavor and texture to your meals.

Consider the creamy richness of a spoonful of almond butter or the satisfying crunch of flaxseeds sprinkled over your morning oatmeal. These small additions can elevate your meals, both nutritionally and taste-wise.

### PLANT-BASED PROTEINS: BEYOND THE BASICS

When we talk about protein in a plant-based diet, we often think of tofu and tempeh, but there's so much more to explore. From seitan to edamame, plant-based proteins are diverse and delicious.

Reflect on the smoky flavor of grilled tempeh in your salad or the tender edamame in your stir-fry. Plant-based proteins can be as flavorful and satisfying as their animal-based counterparts, if not more.

In this chapter, we've taken a closer look at the foods that form the foundation of a plant-based diet. We've seen how each food group - fruits and vegetables, whole grains, legumes, nuts and seeds, and plant-based proteins - contributes to a balanced, nutritious diet. And hopefully, we've sparked excitement in you to explore these foods in your kitchen.

But understanding these foods is just the first step. The

magic happens when you learn to combine them into meals that are not only nourishing but also delicious and satisfying. That's where we'll go next. But for now, take a moment to appreciate the abundance and variety that a plant-based diet offers. The journey is just beginning.

### Plant-Based vs Vegan: The Differences

Let's start by peeling back the layers to understand the nuanced differences between a plant-based diet and a vegan diet.

### Dietary Restrictions

At first glance, both a plant-based diet and a vegan diet seem to share a common principle - excluding animal products from the diet. However, a deeper look reveals distinct differences. A vegan diet rules out all animal products, including meat, dairy, eggs, and even honey. It is strictly plant-focused, leaving no room for animal-derived ingredients.

On the other hand, a plant-based diet emphasizes consuming foods derived from plants. It is flexible, allowing for occasional consumption of animal products based on individual preferences. So, while a vegan diet is a subset of plant-based diets, the reverse is not always true.

### Ethical Considerations

The motivation behind following a vegan or plant-based diet can be different. Many vegans choose this lifestyle for ethical reasons. They object to the use of animals for food, clothing, or any other purpose. This commitment often extends beyond diet to other aspects of life, such as avoiding leather goods and products tested on animals.

Conversely, a plant-based diet is commonly adopted for health reasons. While some plant-based dieters may have ethical motivations, the primary focus is the health benefits of consuming a diet rich in fruits, vegetables, whole grains, and legumes.

### Health Implications

When it comes to health implications, both diets have their merits. A well-planned vegan diet can provide all the nutrients your body needs and may reduce the risk of developing certain diseases. However, because it eliminates all animal products, it requires careful planning to ensure nutritional needs are met, particularly for nutrients like vitamin B12, iron, and omega-3 fatty acids.

In contrast, a plant-based diet, emphasizing whole foods and flexibility to include small amounts of animal products, can make it easier to meet nutritional needs. It also offers the health benefits of consuming a diet high in fiber and low in saturated fats, such as reduced risks of heart disease, obesity, and type 2 diabetes.

### Lifestyle Choices

Finally, it's worth noting that both a vegan and plant-based diet can be part of a broader lifestyle choice. For vegans, this might mean activism for animal rights or making choices that align with cruelty-free and sustainable practices.

On the other hand, those following a plant-based diet might be more focused on personal health and wellness. This could entail regular exercise, mindfulness practices, and a commitment to reducing processed foods in their diet. They may also be motivated by environmental sustainability, as a plant-based diet typically has a smaller ecological footprint compared to a diet high in animal products.

In many ways, the choice between a vegan diet and a plant-based diet is a personal one, reflecting individual values, health goals, and lifestyle preferences. It's not a matter of one being superior to the other but finding what works best for you. Whether you identify as vegan, plant-based, or simply someone trying to eat more fruits and vegetables, the key is to choose a path that aligns with your values and supports your health and well-being.

So, as you move forward, remember there's no one-size-fits-all answer. Your diet should reflect who you are and what you believe in. It's about making choices that feel right for you and respecting that they might look different for others. It's about celebrating the diversity of foods nature provides and the many ways we can enjoy them. Most importantly, it's about nourishing your body with foods that make you feel good, both physically and mentally. That is the essence of a plant-based diet.

### The Health Benefits of Eating Plant-Based

Plant-based diets have been associated with a plethora of health benefits. Let's explore some of these compelling health advantages, which form the heart of a plant-based lifestyle.

#### Heart Health

Plant-based diets have been shown to have significant benefits for heart health. Consuming whole, unprocessed plant foods can lead to lower blood pressure, reduced cholesterol levels, and decreased risk of heart disease. This can be attributed to the high fiber content, the presence of heart-healthy fats, and the lower levels of saturated fats in plant foods compared to animal products.

Consider the avocado, a staple in many plant-based meals. This nutrient-rich fruit is packed with monounsaturated fats, known for their heart-protective properties. A simple avocado toast in the morning or a creamy avocado dressing over your salad can be delicious ways to incorporate these heart-friendly fats into your diet.

### Weight Management

A plant-based diet can be a powerful tool for weight management. Plant foods are typically lower in calories and higher in fiber compared to animal-based foods, making them satisfying and filling. This can help regulate hunger and prevent overeating, leading to natural weight loss without the need for restrictive dieting.

Imagine enjoying a hearty bowl of vegetable soup or a colorful salad before your main meal. These fiber-rich starters can fill you up, reducing the amount of high-calorie foods you might consume afterward. The result? Satisfying meals that aid in weight management without leaving you feeling deprived.

### Diabetes Prevention

Plant-based diets have also been linked to a lower risk of developing type 2 diabetes. High-fiber, low-glycemic foods in a plant-based diet can help regulate blood sugar levels and improve insulin sensitivity. This is crucial in preventing and managing diabetes.

Take the humble lentil, a superstar in plant-based cuisine. Lentils have a low glycemic index, meaning they cause a slow, steady rise in blood sugar instead of a sudden spike. Incorporating lentils into your meals, whether in a hearty stew or a refreshing salad, can be a tasty way to keep your blood sugar levels in check.

### Improved Digestion

As you transition to a plant-based diet, you might notice improvements in your digestion. The high fiber content in plant foods aids in regular bowel movements, preventing constipation and promoting a healthy gut. A healthy digestive system is critical to overall health, as it absorbs nutrients from your food and eliminates waste products from your body.

Visualize starting your day with a bowl of oatmeal topped with fresh fruits. This fiber-packed breakfast can kickstart your digestion, setting the tone for the rest of your day. Remember, a happy gut often means a happy you.

### Enhanced Energy Levels

Many people report increased energy levels when they switch to a plant-based diet. This could be due to the high amounts of vitamins, minerals, and antioxidants in plant foods, which help optimize cellular function and boost energy production.

Think about sipping on a green smoothie for an afternoon pick-me-up instead of reaching for that cup of coffee. Packed with leafy greens, fruits, and a spoonful of nut butter, this energy-boosting snack can provide sustained energy without the caffeine jitters.

Plant-based diets offer a myriad of health benefits, from heart health to weight management, diabetes prevention, improved digestion, and enhanced energy levels. But remember, it's not just about the physical benefits. The peace of mind that comes from knowing you're nourishing your body with wholesome, plant-based foods can be equally rewarding.

Embrace the abundance of fruits, vegetables, whole grains, legumes, nuts, seeds, and plant-based proteins. Explore the myriad of flavors and textures these foods bring to your plate. And enjoy the journey towards better health and well-being. After all, the power of a plant-based diet goes beyond the foods you eat. It's about fostering a deep connection with your food, your body, and the planet. It's about living in a way that nourishes you, heart and soul.

So, please take a deep breath, and let's move forward. There's a world of vibrant, nourishing foods waiting for you. And we're here to explore it together, one delicious bite at a time.

### Sustainability and the Plant-Based Diet
### Reduced Carbon Footprint

A plant-based diet is beneficial not just for our bodies but also for our planet. The food choices we make can significantly impact our carbon footprint. Raising livestock for meat and dairy production contributes to a large percentage of global greenhouse gas emissions. However, by choosing plant-based foods, we can significantly reduce these emissions.

For instance, consider a typical weeknight dinner. You could whip up a beef stir-fry or opt for a tofu stir-fry instead. The beef stir-fry may seem harmless on your plate, but its environmental cost is high. It takes significant resources to raise cattle for beef, including large amounts of feed, water, land, and fuel. This results in high carbon emissions. On the other hand, tofu production requires fewer resources and produces fewer emissions. By choosing the tofu stir-fry, you're effectively reducing your dinner's carbon footprint.

### CONSERVATION OF WATER RESOURCES

In addition to reducing carbon emissions, a plant-based diet can help conserve water resources. Livestock farming is a water-intensive process. It requires substantial amounts of water for animal hydration, crop irrigation, and meat processing. By comparison, growing plants for food generally requires significantly less water.

Think of your breakfast choices. You could have a pair of scrambled eggs or a serving of oatmeal. While both options may satisfy your morning hunger, they impact water resources differently. Producing the eggs requires a large amount of water, from growing the feed for the hens to processing the eggs. In contrast, growing oats and processing them into oatmeal requires less water. By choosing the oatmeal, you're contributing to the conservation of water resources.

### PRESERVATION OF ANIMAL HABITATS

Shifting to a plant-based diet also plays a significant role in preserving animal habitats. Deforestation for livestock farming is a major cause of habitat loss for many species. Reducing the demand for animal products can help slow down deforestation and preserve these habitats.

Imagine your lunch options. You could have a chicken salad or a chickpea salad. The chicken salad may seem like a healthy choice, but its environmental impact is considerable. The land used for raising chickens and growing their feed often comes at the expense of natural habitats. On the other hand, growing chickpeas requires less land and often doesn't necessitate deforestation. By choosing the chickpea salad, you're indirectly helping to preserve animal habitats.

### LOWERING GREENHOUSE GAS EMISSIONS

One of the most significant impacts of a plant-based diet is the potential to lower greenhouse gas emissions. Livestock farming is one of the largest sources of methane, a potent greenhouse gas. By reducing our consumption of animal products, we can help decrease these emissions.

Consider your dessert choices. You could enjoy a slice of cheesecake or apple pie made with vegetable shortening. The cheesecake, while delicious, comes with a high environmental cost. Dairy farming, a major component of cheesecake production, releases significant amounts of methane. On the other hand, an apple pie made with vegetable shortening has a much lower greenhouse gas emission profile. You're playing a part in reducing methane emissions by choosing the apple pie.

While the environmental benefits of a plant-based diet are profound, it's important to remember that it's not about perfection. It's about making more mindful choices when and where we can. It's about recognizing the impact of our food choices and making adjustments that align with our values. It's about understanding that every plant-based meal is a step towards a more sustainable future. And it's about knowing that, together, our small changes can add up to make a big difference.

So, as you fill your plate with colorful fruits, crisp vegetables, hearty grains, protein-packed legumes, and nutrient-dense nuts and seeds, know that you're doing more than just nourishing your body. You're also helping to conserve our planet's precious resources and protect its diverse habitats. You're contributing to a food system that is healthier for us and kinder to our planet. And that is something truly worth celebrating.

# CHAPTER 2

## NUTRITIONAL NEEDS FOR A PLANT-BASED DIET

Take a moment to think of the last meal you had. Was it a bowl of creamy pasta, a crunchy salad, a hearty sandwich, or a comforting bowl of soup? Now, imagine the different components of that meal— the grains, the vegetables, the legumes, the fruits. While delighting your taste buds, each element also works behind the scenes, providing your body with essential nutrients. A meal is more than just a medley of flavors and textures. It's a powerhouse of nutrition, fueling your body and supporting your health.

As we enter the realm of a plant-based diet, understanding the nutritional needs becomes crucial. It's like learning a new language. You start with the alphabet, then move on to words and sentences, and before you know it, you're conversing fluently. Similarly, in the language of nutrition, proteins, vitamins, and minerals are the alphabet. And today, we're starting with the letter 'P' - Protein.

## 2.1 Meeting Your Protein Needs

### Legumes and Lentils

One of the first questions people often ask when considering a plant-based diet is, "Where will I get my protein?" The answer lies in a group of plant foods known as legumes. This includes lentils, chickpeas, black beans, soybeans, and peanuts, to name a few.

Let's take lentils, for instance. A cup of cooked lentils packs about 18 grams of protein. That's roughly equivalent to the protein in three eggs! But unlike eggs, lentils are also high in fiber and low in fat, making them a healthier protein source. Try adding lentils to salads, soups, or curries to boost the protein content of your meals.

### Quinoa and Other Whole Grains

Whole grains are another excellent source of plant-based protein. Not just that, they're also packed with fiber and complex carbohydrates, making them a wholesome addition to your meals.

Think of quinoa, a whole grain often hailed as a superfood. With 8 grams of protein in a cup of cooked quinoa, it's one of the few plant foods that provide all nine essential amino acids, making it a complete protein. You can use quinoa as a base for salads, add it to soups, or even use it to make protein-packed breakfast porridge.

### Nuts and Seeds

Nuts and seeds might be tiny, but they pack a punch for protein. They're also rich in heart-healthy fats and fiber, making them a nutrient-dense snack option.

Picture yourself snacking on a handful of almonds in the afternoon. With 6 grams of protein in a 1-ounce serving, they're a great way to curb hunger and maintain steady energy levels throughout the day. Or imagine starting your day with a bowl of chia seed pudding. With about 5 grams of protein in two tablespoons, chia seeds are a super easy way to boost your protein intake.

Plant-Based Protein Powders

While whole foods should be the primary source of protein in a plant-based diet, protein powders can also be a convenient way to ensure you're meeting your protein needs. They're convenient for those with increased protein requirements, like athletes or those recovering from an illness or surgery.

Consider adding a scoop of plant-based protein powder to your morning smoothie. It could be a pea and brown rice protein blend, providing a complete amino acid profile. Or it could be a hemp protein powder, boasting protein, fiber, and healthy fats. Just remember to choose a protein powder low in sugar and free from artificial additives.

Learning to meet your protein needs on a plant-based diet is like learning how to ride a bike. It might seem challenging initially, but it becomes second nature with some practice. And just like riding a bike opens up a world of possibilities, mastering your protein needs allows you to harness the full potential of a plant-based diet. So explore the power of plant-based proteins, and let them fuel your journey towards health and vitality.

## 2.2 Vitamins and Minerals: Getting Enough

### Vitamin B12 from Fortified Foods

In the symphony of nutrition, each vitamin and mineral plays a unique and vital role. Take Vitamin B12, a critical player that keeps our body's nerve and blood cells healthy. It also helps prevent anemia that can make people tired and weak. The primary sources of Vitamin B12 are animal products, which poses a question for those following a plant-based diet. Where do we get our B12?

The answer is fortified foods. These are foods that have been enriched with essential nutrients. Many plant milks, breakfast cereals, and soy products are fortified with B12. An easy way to incorporate these into your diet could be a bowl of fortified cereal with plant milk for breakfast or a lunchtime stir-fry with fortified tofu. By including these foods in your daily meals, you can ensure your body gets the B12 it needs to stay healthy.

### Calcium from Leafy Greens

Calcium is next on our nutritional tour, famous for supporting strong bones and teeth. But did you know it also plays a crucial role in heart, muscle, and nerve function? Most people get their calcium from dairy products, but leafy greens are an excellent source for those on a plant-based diet.

Think of foods like kale, collard greens, and bok choy. These leafy greens are rich in calcium and can be easily added to your meals. Picture a dinner of stir-fried bok choy with garlic or a lunch of kale salad with a tangy dressing. These dishes are delicious and help you meet your calcium needs.

Iron from Lentils and Chickpeas

Iron is another vital nutrient essential for producing red blood cells and transporting oxygen throughout the body. While meat is often touted as the best iron source, plenty of plant-based sources are available.

Lentils and chickpeas, for example, are excellent sources of iron. A cup of cooked lentils provides about 37% of your daily iron needs. Similarly, a cup of cooked chickpeas provides about 26% of daily needs. Imagine a comforting lentil soup for a chilly evening or a refreshing chickpea salad on a warm afternoon. These meals not only satisfy your taste buds but also provide a good dose of iron.

Omega-3 from Flaxseeds and Chia Seeds

Last but not least, let's talk about Omega-3 fatty acids. These are essential fats that have significant benefits for heart and brain health. Flaxseeds and chia seeds are the best plant-based sources of these essential fats.

One tablespoon of flaxseeds or chia seeds provides enough Omega-3 fatty acids. You can sprinkle ground flaxseeds or chia seeds on your breakfast cereal, add them to your smoothies, or use them as a topping for salads. It's an easy and tasty way to incorporate these heart-healthy fats into your diet.

Each meal is a new opportunity to nourish your body with essential vitamins and minerals in a plant-based diet.

Choosing various nutrient-rich foods ensures your body gets all the nutrients it needs to function optimally. And as you explore the world of plant-based nutrition, remember that it's about more than just eating plants. It's about fueling your body with the best nature offers and honoring your health with every bite.

Like a well-orchestrated symphony, a balanced plant-based diet combines different elements to create a harmonious whole. Each nutrient, each food, and each meal plays a part in this beautiful composition. So, here's to the joy of plant-based eating, the beauty of balance, and the power of nutrition.

### 2.3 Understanding Food Labels

#### Identifying Plant-Based Ingredients

Imagine standing in the grocery store, a new product in hand. You flip it over and scan the list of ingredients. You spot familiar names like tomatoes, whole wheat flour, and olive oil. But then, there are others that sound like they belong in a chemistry lab rather than in your food. How do you decipher this code and determine if the product aligns with your plant-based lifestyle?

The first step is to look for ingredients you recognize — fruits, vegetables, grains, legumes, nuts, and seeds. These are the building blocks of a plant-based diet. If you see these ingredients at the beginning of the list, it's a good sign. The order of ingredients on a label reflects their proportion in the product, with the highest quantity of ingredients listed first.

Next, look for plant-based proteins like soy, lentils, chickpeas, or pea protein. If you spot these, you're on the right track. Other plant-based ingredients to look for include whole grains (like brown rice, oats, or quinoa), natural sweeteners (like maple syrup or dates), and heart-healthy fats (like avocados or chia seeds).

Spotting Hidden Animal Products

Unfortunately, not all ingredient lists are straightforward. Some products may seem plant-based at first glance but contain hidden animal-derived ingredients. These can sneak into your foods as additives or flavorings, often under scientific names.

For instance, casein and whey are milk proteins often found in "non-dairy" products. Gelatin, derived from animal bones and skin, can lurk in gummy candies and marshmallows. Carmine, a red dye made from insects, is used in some red-colored foods and cosmetics. Even certain types of Vitamin D3 can be animal-derived.

Learning to spot these hidden animal products can take a bit of practice. A quick internet search can help clarify unfamiliar ingredients. There are also smartphone apps available that can scan a product's barcode and instantly tell you if it's vegan.

Recognizing Nutritional Information

Beyond the ingredient list, food labels also provide a snapshot of the product's nutritional content. This can be a valuable tool for ensuring your plant-based diet is nutritionally balanced.

Pay attention to the serving size first. All the nutritional information on the label is based on this amount. Then, look at the calories per serving. If you're managing your weight, this information can be beneficial.

Next, check the amounts of macronutrients — carbohydrates, proteins, and fats. A balanced plant-based diet should include a good mix of all three. Also, take note of the fiber content. Plant-based diets are typically high in fiber, which is beneficial for digestive health.

Lastly, look at the vitamins and minerals. These micronutrients are essential for various bodily functions. Key ones to look for include Vitamin B12, Vitamin D, calcium, iron, and zinc. If these are present in significant amounts, it's a bonus.

Deciphering Food Additives

Food additives can be particularly tricky to decipher. These are substances added to foods to improve their shelf life, taste, texture, or appearance. Some are plant-based, some are animal-derived, and some can be either.

For instance, lecithin, an emulsifier used in many processed foods, can be derived from soy (plant-based) or eggs (not plant-based). Similarly, mono- and diglycerides, used to improve food texture, can be derived from plant or animal fats. Other common additives include various types of gums (like xanthan gum or guar gum), typically plant-based, and natural flavors, which can be plant-based or animal-derived.

While some food additives are harmless, others may have adverse health effects or be inconsistent with a plant-based lifestyle. As a rule of thumb, if a product's ingredient list is long and filled with additives you don't recognize, it's probably not the healthiest choice.

Understanding food labels is a bit like detective work. It involves scanning for clues, deciphering codes, and spotting red herrings. But it can become a routine part of your shopping experience with practice. And the reward is worth it — the peace of mind that comes with knowing exactly what's in your food. So, next time you're in the grocery store, take a moment to flip over that package and embark on a bit of detective work. Your health and your planet will thank you.

## 2.4 Supplements: Do You Need Them?

As we navigate the path of plant-based nutrition, it's important to remember that while whole foods are the stars of the show, sometimes a supporting cast is needed. Just as a beautiful garden might need extra watering during a dry spell, your body might need supplemental nourishment during your transition to plant-based eating. Supplements can be valuable in ensuring your body's nutritional needs are met. Let's explore some essential supplements you might consider incorporating into your plant-based lifestyle.

### Vitamin B12 Supplements

Think of Vitamin B12 as the conductor of your body's orchestra, coordinating the symphony of cells in your body to create the music of health. This vital nutrient plays a crucial role in nerve function, the creation of DNA, and the formation of red blood cells. While Vitamin B12 can be found in fortified foods, it's naturally present in significant amounts, mostly in animal products.

A Vitamin B12 supplement can be an insurance policy for

those following a plant-based diet, ensuring your body gets enough of this essential nutrient. The daily recommended amount for most adults is 2.4 micrograms, which can easily be met with a supplement. And because Vitamin B12 is water-soluble, your body naturally excretes any excess, so there's little risk of toxicity.

<u>Omega-3 Fatty Acid Supplements</u>

Next on our list of potential supplements are Omega-3 fatty acids. These are the good guys, the heart-friendly fats that support brain health, reduce inflammation, and may even improve your mood. While flaxseeds and chia seeds are excellent plant-based sources of Omega-3s, they provide a type called ALA, which needs to be converted by your body into the active forms of EPA and DHA.

However, this conversion process can be inefficient so that supplements can be helpful. Look for algae-based supplements, which provide a direct source of EPA and DHA, bypassing the need for your body to do the conversion.

<u>Iron Supplements</u>

Iron plays a starring role in your body's production of red blood cells and in carrying oxygen to your body's tissues. While there are plenty of plant-based sources of iron, the type of iron found in plants (non-heme iron) is not as easily absorbed by your body as the type found in animal products (heme iron).

To help your body absorb the iron from plant foods, pair them with Vitamin C-rich foods like oranges, strawberries, or bell peppers. However, suppose you're finding it challenging to meet your iron needs through food alone. In that case, you might consider an iron supplement, particularly if you're an individual with higher iron needs, like athletes or menstruating.

<u>Vitamin D Supplements</u>

Our final potential supplement is Vitamin D, the sunshine vitamin because our bodies can produce it when our skin is exposed to sunlight. Vitamin D supports bone health and immune function and may help prevent depression. However, for those living in northern latitudes or who don't get much sun exposure, getting enough Vitamin D can be a challenge.

While some mushrooms and fortified foods provide a form of Vitamin D, it may not be sufficient to meet your body's needs. In this case, a Vitamin D supplement, specifically Vitamin D3, can benefit your diet.

Supplements can be considered the finishing touches to your plant-based diet, like adding a splash of color to a painting or a pinch of salt to a dish. They're not a substitute for a diet rich in whole, plant-based foods, but they can serve as a safety net, ensuring that your nutritional bases are covered.

As you continue to explore the world of plant-based nutrition, remember that everybody and their nutritional needs are unique. What works for one person might not work for another. Listen to your body, and don't hesitate to seek guidance from a healthcare provider or a registered dietitian. After all, a plant-based diet is about what you eat and how you nourish your body and mind.

So, armed with knowledge and motivated by the vision of

better health, let's continue to cultivate the garden of plant-based nutrition. Let's continue to explore, to learn, to grow. And most importantly, let's continue celebrating the delicious simplicity and profound wisdom of plant-based eating. Onward to the next step on this exciting path.

# CHAPTER 3

## SETTING UP YOUR PLANT-BASED KITCHEN

Imagine walking into a painter's studio. Canvases are neatly stacked against the wall, tubes of paint organized by color, brushes of all sizes in jars, and the air is filled with the scent of paint and endless possibilities. Now, envision your kitchen in a similar light - a studio where you, the artist, create nourishing meals that are works of art for the palate. Like the painter needs her brushes and paints, you need kitchen equipment to bring your plant-based creations to life.

Stepping into a well-equipped kitchen can feel empowering, like stepping into a superhero's suit. You're ready to take on any recipe, confident you have the tools to turn a handful of ingredients into a delicious meal. So, let's put on our capes and transform your kitchen into a plant-based haven, starting with the essential kitchen equipment.

### 3.1 Essential Kitchen Equipment

#### HIGH-SPEED BLENDER

A high-speed blender is like the power drill in your kitchen tool kit. It's versatile, powerful, and can significantly speed up your meal preparation. From creating creamy plant-based milk and smoothies to blending soups and sauces, a high-speed blender is a must-have in a plant-based kitchen.

Imagine waking up to a refreshing green smoothie packed with fruits, leafy greens, and a scoop of plant-based protein powder. You can whip up this nutrient-rich breakfast in minutes with a high-speed blender. Or think about preparing a creamy cashew sauce for a pasta dish. Your high-speed blender can turn soaked cashews into a velvety smooth sauce, adding a touch of decadence to your meal.

#### FOOD PROCESSOR

Next on our list is the food processor, the sous chef of your kitchen. It can chop, slice, shred, and grind, saving time and effort. Whether you're making a chunky salsa, a smooth hummus, or a hearty nut loaf, a food processor can handle it all.

Consider the task of chopping vegetables for a stir-fry. With a food processor, you can chop your veggies in a fraction of the time it would take to do it by hand. Or imagine making a batch of homemade veggie burgers. Your food processor can quickly grind the beans, vegetables, and spices, creating a burger mix with the perfect texture.

#### GOOD-QUALITY KNIVES

A set of good-quality knives is as essential to a chef as a paintbrush is to a painter. A sharp knife can make the task safer, faster, and more enjoyable, from dicing an onion to chopping a butternut squash.

Think about prepping a salad. A sharp knife can easily slice through ripe tomatoes, crisp cucumbers, and crunchy bell peppers, ensuring your ingredients maintain their shape and texture. Or consider the task of mincing garlic for a stir-fry. A good knife can turn a whole clove of garlic into fine mince in seconds, releasing its aromatic flavors.

**VARIETY OF POTS AND PANS**

Finally, various pots and pans can be likened to the canvas for your culinary creations. Different meals require different types of cookware, and a variety ensures you're ready for any recipe.

Picture yourself simmering a pot of lentil soup on a cold winter day. A large, heavy-bottomed pot is perfect for distributing the heat evenly and allowing the flavors to meld together beautifully. Or think about sautéing vegetables for a stir-fry. A wide, shallow pan allows the vegetables to cook quickly and evenly without steaming.

In the grand scheme of plant-based cooking, your kitchen equipment plays a starring role. Like an artist's tools, they help you bring your vision to life, transforming simple ingredients into delicious meals. So equip your kitchen with these essentials, and let them empower you on your plant-based journey. Remember, the only limit is your creativity. So, go on, unleash your inner chef, and let the magic unfold.

3.2 Building Your Plant-Based Pantry

A well-stocked pantry is like having a treasure chest brimming with gems that can transform into nourishing, delicious meals. It's the backbone of your kitchen, providing the staples you'll need to whip up plant-based dishes quickly. Let's explore the critical components of a plant-based pantry.

### Whole Grains and Pasta

Whole grains are the sturdy anchors of many plant-based meals. They are rich in fiber, protein, and many essential nutrients. Imagine the nutty flavor of brown rice paired with a stir-fry, the hearty texture of barley in a comforting soup, or the delicate, fluffy quinoa as a base for your favorite salad.

In addition to whole grains, pasta - from spaghetti to penne to fusilli - also merits a spot in your pantry. Go for whole grain varieties when possible, but don't forget that pasta made from legumes adds even more protein. Picture unwinding after a long day with a bowl of pasta tossed in a vibrant plant-based sauce - simple, comforting, and utterly satisfying.

### Canned and Dried Legumes

Legumes are the star players of the plant-based protein team. From lentils and chickpeas to black beans and peas, they're versatile, delicious, and packed with nutrients. Dried legumes are cost-effective and can be prepared in batches for convenient use. Picture a pot of chili simmering on the stove, featuring a trio of beans you had ready in your pantry.

Canned legumes, on the other hand, are perfect when you need a quick meal. Imagine whipping a chickpea curry on a busy weeknight or a black bean taco filling in a pinch. Having a variety of canned and dried legumes on hand ensures that a protein-rich meal is never more than a few steps away.

### Variety of Nuts and Seeds

Nuts and seeds are flavorful accessories that add a crunch and essential nutrients to your meals. Almonds, walnuts, chia seeds, flaxseeds - each brings a unique profile of healthy fats, protein, and other nutrients. Picture a salad sprinkled with toasted walnuts or a creamy smoothie boosted with a spoonful of chia seeds.

Moreover, nuts and seeds can be transformed into delicious plant-based milk and butter. Imagine the gratification of pouring homemade almond milk into your morning coffee or spreading freshly made peanut butter onto a slice of whole-grain bread.

### SPICES AND HERBS

Spices and herbs are the magic wands of your kitchen, capable of turning the simplest ingredients into a feast for the senses. From the warmth of cinnamon in a breakfast porridge to the smoky flavor of paprika in a vegetable sauté or the refreshing note of basil in a summer salad - they can elevate your meals to new culinary heights.

In addition to their flavor-enhancing qualities, many spices and herbs also boast impressive health benefits. For instance, turmeric is known for its anti-inflammatory effects, while cinnamon can help regulate blood sugar levels. So, stock your pantry with various spices and herbs, and let them work their magic on your meals.

### PLANT-BASED MILK AND SAUCES

Lastly, plant-based milks and sauces are versatile accomplices that add finishing touches to your meals. Whether it's a splash of soy milk in your tea, a drizzle of tahini sauce on your salad, or a dollop of marinara on your pizza - they can enhance your dishes' flavor, texture, and nutritional profile.

When choosing plant-based milk, go for unsweetened versions whenever possible. As for sauces, opt for those with minimal added sugars and preservatives. Better yet, try making your own. Imagine the delight of tasting your homemade marinara sauce, knowing exactly what went into it, or the satisfaction of creating your almond milk, free from any additives.

Your pantry is the canvas on which you'll paint your plant-based meals. By stocking it with a variety of whole grains, legumes, nuts and seeds, spices and herbs, and plant-based milks and sauces, you'll ensure that you have the palette of ingredients needed to create vibrant, nourishing, and delicious meals. So, let's open the doors to your plant-based pantry and let the culinary creations begin.

### 3.3 Shopping for Plant-Based Foods

#### SEASONAL PRODUCE

Every venture into the grocery store, or perhaps a local farmer's market, can be a delightful exploration of colors, textures, and flavors that Mother Nature has to offer. And the most vibrant, succulent, and nutrient-dense of the lot are often the fruits and vegetables currently in season. Like nature's calendar, the rotating availability of various produce can guide what to put on your plate at different times of the year.

Imagine the crispness of a freshly harvested apple in the fall, the tangy burst of a ripe orange in the winter, the refreshing bite of a cucumber in the summer, or the sweet tenderness of a cherry in the spring. You can enjoy your fruits and vegetables at their peak taste and nutritional value by choosing seasonal produce. Plus, it's a great way to support local farming communities and reduce your environmental impact.

### Bulk Buying for Grains and Legumes

Next, focus on the aisles filled with whole grains and legumes. These nutrient powerhouses form the base of many plant-based meals and are often available in bulk, which can be a cost-effective and eco-friendly shopping strategy.

Consider the humble chickpea, a versatile legume that can be transformed into many dishes, from comforting curries to crunchy roasted snacks. Or contemplate the versatile oats, waiting to be morphed into a warm morning porridge, a batch of homemade granola, or even a nourishing face mask. By purchasing these staples in bulk, you can always have your go-to ingredients on hand while saving money and reducing packaging waste.

### Choosing Organic Options

As you navigate the grocery store or market, you might also encounter foods labeled 'organic.' Organic foods are grown without synthetic pesticides, fertilizers, genetically modified organisms, or irradiation. While the jury is still out on whether organic foods are nutritionally superior to conventional ones, choosing organic can reduce your exposure to chemical residues and support farming practices that are more sustainable and kinder to our planet.

Consider the leafy spinach, one of the crops that is often heavily sprayed with pesticides. Organic spinach can be a healthier choice for you and the environment. However, remember that not all produce needs to be bought organic. As a rule of thumb, consider opting for organic when buying the 'Dirty Dozen' (the twelve fruits and vegetables that tend to have the highest pesticide residues) and save your pennies on the 'Clean Fifteen' (those that typically have the least pesticide residues.)

### Exploring Farmers Markets

Lastly, let's step outside the traditional grocery store and venture into the bustling, vibrant world of farmers' markets. Here, you'll find a cornucopia of fresh, locally grown produce, often picked at the peak of ripeness and bursting with flavor and nutrients.

Imagine the smell of fresh herbs, the sight of colorful vegetables, the sound of friendly chatter, and the feel of a juicy peach in your hand. Shopping at farmers' markets is not just a chore but a sensory-rich experience that anchors us to the seasons, the community, and the land that feeds us. Plus, it's an opportunity to meet the people who grow your food and learn about the love and labor that goes into each harvest.

So, equip yourself with a few reusable bags and head to your local farmers' market. You might discover a new type of vegetable, taste the sweetest tomato, or enjoy a sense of connection to your food and community.

In the world of plant-based eating, grocery shopping is not just a mundane task but an opportunity to explore, discover, and make choices that align with your health and values. It's about filling your cart with vibrant fruits and vegetables, hearty grains and legumes, and a sprinkle of conscious choices. So, put on your shopping shoes, grab your grocery list, and let's head out to the grocery store. The aisles of possibilities await.

### 3.4 Food Storage Tips

#### PROPER REFRIGERATION

A well-organized refrigerator is like a well-oiled machine, humming along efficiently, keeping your food fresh and safe. Each section of your refrigerator has different temperature zones, making it ideal for specific types of food.

The coldest part is usually the back of the lower shelf, perfect for storing plant-based milk, fresh juices, and cooked leftovers. The crisper drawers maintain a humid environment ideal for fresh fruits and vegetables. Remember to keep them separate, as certain fruits emit a gas that can speed up the ripening process of vegetables.

Your refrigerator door is the warmest part and should be reserved for condiments, pickles, and other foods less prone to spoiling.

#### USING GLASS CONTAINERS FOR STORAGE

Once you've prepared a delicious plant-based meal, storing leftovers properly is key to maintaining their quality and safety. Enter glass containers - the superheroes of food storage. They are non-reactive, meaning they won't leach any chemicals into your food, even when reheating. Plus, they're dishwasher safe and do not retain any food stains or odors.

Storing leftovers in glass containers with tight-fitting lids keeps food fresh and prevents spills. And because they're transparent, you can easily see what's inside, making meal planning a breeze. For instance, yesterday's vegetable stir-fry can be today's lunch, and the leftover chickpea curry can be repurposed into a delicious filling for wraps.

### Freezing Fresh Produce

Sometimes, despite our best planning, we end up with more fresh produce than we can use. Freezing is a fantastic way to extend the shelf-life of these foods and prevent waste.

Most fruits freeze well and can be used later in smoothies, baking, or cooking. Berries can be frozen directly on a tray, while larger fruits like bananas and peaches should be sliced before freezing.

Many vegetables benefit from a quick blanching before freezing to preserve their color and texture. Immerse them in boiling water for a few minutes, then transfer them to an ice bath to halt the cooking process. Pat dry and freeze in single layers on a tray before transferring to freezer bags or containers.

### Storing Grains and Legumes

Grains and legumes are the workhorses of a plant-based kitchen, and storing them correctly ensures they're always ready to be turned into a hearty meal.

These pantry staples should be kept in airtight containers in a cool, dark place. This keeps out moisture and pests and maintains their freshness. Whole grains and legumes can be stored for several months. Once cooked, they should be stored in the refrigerator and consumed within a few days.

Your food storage practices play a crucial role in maintaining the quality and safety of your plant-based foods. So, take a moment to appreciate the harmony in your well-organized refrigerator, the simplicity of your neatly stacked glass containers, the bounty in your freezer, and the promise held in the jars of grains and legumes in your pantry. Each component, each step, is a testament to your commitment to nourishing yourself with the best that plant-based eating has to offer.

And with that, our tour of a plant-based kitchen ends. But remember, this is just the beginning. Your kitchen and pantry are now a playground waiting for you to explore, experiment, and create. So, roll up your sleeves, put on your apron, and let's get cooking!

# CHAPTER 4

## THE ABCS OF PLANT-BASED COOKING

Imagine stepping into an artist's studio. The smell of paint, the array of brushes, the spectrum of colors, all ready to be transformed into a masterpiece. Now, think about your kitchen. Just as an artist uses different techniques to bring their artwork to life, you'll need to master various cooking techniques to create your plant-based masterpieces. Welcome to the studio of your plant-based kitchen. It's time to pick up your whisk, put on your apron, and get ready to create some culinary art!

4.1 Basic Cooking Techniques

Steaming Vegetables

Just as watercolors allow the texture of the paper to shine through, steaming vegetables let their natural flavor and color take center stage. It's a gentle cooking method that preserves the crispness and nutrients of the vegetables.

You'll need a pot with a tight-fitting lid and a steamer basket to steam vegetables. Add a couple of inches of water to the pot, insert the basket, and bring the water to a boil. Add your vegetables, cover the pot, and let the steam work magic. The cooking time will depend on the type and size of the vegetables. For example, broccoli florets might take around 5 minutes, while whole artichokes could take up to 40 minutes.

## Cooking Grains

Cooking grains is like preparing a canvas for a painting. It provides a base on which to layer flavors and textures. Each type of grain has its unique cooking method and water ratio, but the basic steps remain the same.

Start by rinsing the grains under cold water to remove dust or impurities. Add the grains and water to a pot. As a general rule, use two parts water to one part grain, but this can vary depending on the type of grain. Bring the water to a boil, then reduce the heat to low, cover the pot, and let the grains simmer until they absorb all the water. Let them sit, covered, for a few minutes after turning off the heat to steam a bit. This will make them fluffier.

## Preparing Legumes

Preparing legumes is like developing a photograph. It's a process that transforms a raw, hard bean into a tender, digestible, and nutritious food. You can either cook dried legumes or use canned ones.

If you're using dried legumes, you'll need to soak them first. This reduces their cooking time and makes them easier to digest. Place the legumes in a large bowl, cover them with plenty of water, and let them soak. Most legumes need to be soaked for 8 hours or overnight, but some, like lentils and split peas, don't need to be soaked.

Once the legumes are soaked, rinse them and transfer them to a pot. Cover them with water, boil them, then reduce the heat and let them simmer until they're tender. The cooking time will depend on the type and age of the legumes.

If you're using canned legumes, the process is even more straightforward. Just open the can, drain, and rinse the legumes, and they're ready to use!

<u>Roasting Vegetables</u>

Roasting is to vegetables what sunlight is to a landscape - it intensifies colors, deepens flavors, and brings out hidden details. It's a simple technique that can transform even the humblest vegetable into a mouthwatering side dish.

To roast vegetables, start by preheating your oven. Most vegetables roast well at high temperatures, around 425°F (220°C). Cut your vegetables into even pieces, toss them with oil, and spread them out on a baking sheet. Don't overcrowd the pan, as this can cause the vegetables to steam instead of roast.

Put the pan in the oven and let the vegetables roast until they're tender and slightly caramelized. The cooking time will depend on the type and size of the vegetables. For example, diced potatoes might take around 30 minutes, while asparagus might be done in 15 minutes. Turn the vegetables once or twice during roasting to ensure they cook evenly.

Now that you're equipped with these fundamental cooking techniques, you can start creating your plant-based masterpieces. Remember, cooking is an art; like any art, it takes practice. Don't be afraid to experiment, make mistakes, and learn as you go. After all, every great artist was once a beginner. So, embrace the process, enjoy the journey, and let your kitchen be your canvas. Happy cooking!

### 4.2 Prepping Your Ingredients

#### Washing and Cutting Vegetables

The first thing to remember when preparing vegetables is that cleanliness is vital. A thorough wash can remove any dirt, bacteria, and traces of pesticides from the surface, ensuring your veggies are safe for consumption. Use a gentle, steady stream of cold water and a soft brush for stubborn dirt, especially on root vegetables like potatoes and carrots.

Once your vegetables are clean, it's time to wield your knife. How you cut your vegetables can affect their cooking time and final texture. For example, thinly slicing a carrot will result in a quicker cooking time and a softer texture than chopping it into larger chunks.

Use a stable cutting surface when cutting vegetables, and take your time. And don't forget about safety: always cut away from your body and keep your fingers clear of the blade.

#### Soaking Legumes and Grains

Next up are legumes and grains, two cornerstones of plant-based cooking. While canned legumes are ready to use, dried legumes need some prep work. Soaking not only speeds up their cooking time but can also make them easier to digest.

Place legumes in a large bowl and cover them with plenty

of water to soak them. Most legumes need to soak for about eight hours or overnight, but smaller ones like lentils and split peas can be soaked for a shorter time.

Some grains, like quinoa and buckwheat, also benefit from soaking. This helps to soften their texture and can make them easier to digest. Soaking grains for just a few hours can be enough, but they can also be soaked overnight.

<u>Marinating Tofu</u>

Tofu is a plant-based protein superstar. But before it can shine in your dishes, it might need a little pampering in the form of marinating. Marinating not only infuses tofu with flavor but can also enhance its texture.

To marinate tofu, start by pressing it to remove excess water. This allows it to absorb the marinade better. Then, cut your tofu into slices, cubes, or whatever shape suits your recipe.

Whisk together your marinade ingredients in a bowl. This could be a simple soy sauce and olive oil mix or a more complex blend of spices, herbs, and other flavorings. Add the tofu to the marinade and let it soak for at least 30 minutes or up to a day.

<u>Prepping Nuts and Seeds</u>

The final stop in our ingredient prep tour is the nuts and seeds station. These little powerhouses are packed with nutrients and can add a satisfying meal crunch.

Before using nuts and seeds, consider giving them a quick toast. This enhances their flavor and makes them even more delicious. Spread them on a baking sheet and toast them in a

350°F (175°C) oven for 10-15 minutes or until they're lightly golden and fragrant.

Remember, each ingredient you prepare is a stroke of your culinary brush, a note in your food symphony. The care and attention you put into prepping your ingredients will shine through in your finished dishes. So, enjoy the process and know you're creating something special with each chop, soak, marinate, and toast.

## 4.3 Understanding Cooking Times

### Grains and Legumes

In plant-based cuisine, grains and legumes are the backbone of many dishes, from hearty stews to refreshing salads. But to bring these ingredients to their full potential, understanding their cooking times is paramount.

Consider the process of cooking lentils. Depending on the variety, these versatile legumes typically take about 15 to 20 minutes to cook. Red lentils cook faster, while green and brown lentils take longer. The result? Perfectly tender lentils that are ready to be transformed into a comforting soup or a vibrant salad.

On the other hand, grains like brown rice require a longer cooking time. A cup of brown rice can take up to 45 minutes to cook, resulting in a fluffy, nutty grain that can serve as a base for your stir-fry or a filling for your burritos.

So, the next time you plan to cook grains or legumes, take a moment to consider their cooking times. This will help you plan your meals better and ensure that your ingredients are cooked to perfection.

### Roasting Vegetables

Roasting is a cooking technique that can unlock a bounty of flavors in your vegetables, transforming them into caramelized, tender delights. However, it's crucial to remember that not all vegetables are created equal when roasting.

For instance, root vegetables like potatoes, carrots, and beets are denser and take longer to roast. Depending on their size, these hearty veggies might need up to an hour in the oven.

Conversely, softer vegetables like bell peppers, zucchini, and tomatoes roast much quicker. These tender vegetables might only need 15 to 20 minutes in the oven to reach their sweet, roasted best.

By understanding the cooking times of different vegetables, you can orchestrate your roasting process to ensure that everything comes out of the oven at its best, ready to grace your plate with its roasted goodness.

Steaming Greens

Steaming is a cooking method that allows the natural beauty of your greens to shine. It's a gentle technique that preserves your leafy vegetables' vibrant color and delicate texture, making them a pleasure to eat.

When it comes to steaming greens, timing is everything. Spinach, with its tender leaves, might need just a minute or two to wilt to perfection. On the other hand, heartier greens like kale or collard might require a bit more time, around 5 to 7 minutes, to reach their tender best.

So, when you're ready to steam your greens, watch the

clock. A perfectly steamed green is a treat for the senses, a vibrant addition to your plant-based meals.

Baking Plant-Based Desserts

When baking plant-based desserts, understanding your cooking times can be the difference between a gooey brownie and a dry piece of cake. Baking is a science, and each recipe has its unique formula, including the baking time.

Consider a tray of vegan chocolate chip cookies. These sweet treats might need around 10 to 12 minutes in the oven to achieve a crispy edge and a soft center. Leave them in for too long, and you might end up with cookies that are too hard. Take them out too soon; they might be too soft and undercooked.

On the other hand, a vegan apple pie might need up to an hour in the oven, allowing the apples to soften and the crust to become golden brown and flaky.

So, whether you're whipping up a batch of muffins or a decadent cake, always pay attention to the cooking time. It's one of the key elements to creating delicious, plant-based desserts that everyone will love.

In the orchestra of your plant-based kitchen, cooking times are the rhythm section, keeping everything in sync and harmony. By understanding the unique cooking times of different ingredients, you can create meals that hit all the right notes. So, keep your timer handy, listen to the rhythm of your kitchen, and let the culinary symphony play on!

4.4 Making Your Meals Flavorful

Using Fresh Herbs

Imagine stepping into a garden, vibrant with a variety of

herbs. There's the sweet aroma of basil, the fresh scent of mint, the earthy smell of rosemary, and the warm fragrance of thyme. Each herb, with its unique aroma and flavor, adds a layer of complexity and freshness to your dishes.

An herb-infused tomato sauce, for instance, can elevate a simple pasta dish. A sprinkle of parsley or cilantro can add freshness to a salad or soup. Chopped basil can turn a piece of toasted bread and fresh tomatoes into a gourmet delight.

When using fresh herbs, add them towards the end of the cooking process. This preserves their aroma and color and keeps their delicate flavors intact. Remember, when it comes to herbs, less is often more. Start with a small amount and add more as needed.

<u>Incorporating Spices</u>

The world of spices is like a box of colored pencils, each spice adding a different hue and depth to your dish. From the warm sweetness of cinnamon to the smoky heat of paprika, the earthy flavor of cumin, to the vibrant color of turmeric, each spice has a story to tell.

A dash of ground cumin can add a layer of warmth and richness to a lentil soup. A sprinkle of cinnamon can transform a bowl of oatmeal into a comforting breakfast. A pinch of turmeric can give a vibrant color and a subtle depth to a pot of rice.

When using spices, feel free to experiment and create your own blends. Toasting the spices before grinding them can intensify their flavors. And remember, spices have a shelf life. Over time, they lose their potency and flavor. So, make sure your spices are fresh to get the most out of them.

### Adding Umami Flavors

Umami, often described as a savory taste, is like the bass notes in a piece of music. It gives depth and body to your dishes. Ingredients like soy sauce, miso, and nutritional yeast are rich in umami flavors and can be great additions to your plant-based meals.

A spoonful of miso can add a savory depth to a vegetable broth. A sprinkle of nutritional yeast can give a cheesy flavor to a pasta dish without any dairy. A dash of soy sauce can enhance the flavors of a stir-fry or a marinade.

Incorporating umami flavors into your meals can make them more satisfying and fulfilling. It's like adding a dollop of magic that transforms a simple dish into an exquisite culinary experience.

### Balancing Sweet, Sour, Salty, and Bitter Tastes

Creating a balance of tastes in your dishes is like composing a piece of music. You have the sweetness from ripe fruits or root vegetables, the sourness from citrus fruits or vinegar, the saltiness from sea salt or soy sauce, and the bitterness from leafy greens or certain herbs.

A successful dish often has a balance of these tastes. For instance, a salad dressing with maple syrup's sweetness, lemon juice's sourness, and sea salt's saltiness creates a harmonious blend of flavors. A stir-fry with the bitterness of broccoli, bell peppers' sweetness, pineapple's sourness, and soy sauce's saltiness results in a flavorful and satisfying dish.

As you cook, taste your food and adjust the flavors as needed. Remember, the goal is not to have all tastes in equal amounts but to create a harmonious blend that makes your taste buds dance with joy.

As you continue to create your culinary masterpieces, remember that each ingredient, technique, and flavor is a note in your symphony, a stroke in your painting, or a thread in your tapestry. You're not just cooking food; you're creating art. Art that nourishes your body delights your senses and celebrates the abundance of plant-based eating. So, keep exploring, experimenting, and creating because your kitchen is your studio, and you are the artist. Now, let's turn the page and discover the vibrant world of plant-based recipes together.

# CHAPTER 5

## RISE AND SHINE: PLANT-BASED BREAKFASTS TO KICK START YOUR DAY

Picture this: it's a tranquil morning, and the day begins to unfurl. The sun is casting long, golden rays through your kitchen window, and the aroma of freshly brewed coffee is wafting through the air. You're about to create a breakfast that nourishes your body and delights your taste buds. Welcome to the first meal of the day, where we explore the wonderful world of plant-based breakfasts.

Breakfast is often hailed as the most important meal of the day and for a good reason. It breaks your overnight fast, kick-starts your metabolism, and provides the energy you need to tackle the day. A well-balanced, plant-based breakfast can set the tone for a day of healthful eating. So, let's begin this beautiful morning with a classic favorite: pancakes. But these aren't your ordinary pancakes; these are whole-grain pancakes served with a delightful berry compote.

### 5.1 WHOLE GRAIN PANCAKES WITH BERRY COMPOTE

*(Serves four people, 200-250 cal/serving, two pancakes. Whole grain flour is rich in dietary fiber, vitamins, and minerals).*

<u>Whole Grain Pancake Preparation</u>

Whole-grain pancakes are the superheroes of the breakfast table. Packed with fiber and other essential nutrients, these pancakes will keep you satiated and energized throughout the morning. Here's a simple recipe to get you started:

- 1 cup whole grain flour (like whole wheat or oat flour)

- 1 tablespoon baking powder
- 1/4 teaspoon salt
- 1 cup plant-based milk
- 1 tablespoon maple syrup
- 1 teaspoon vanilla extract

Combine the flour, baking powder, and salt in a large bowl. Whisk together the plant-based milk, maple syrup, and vanilla extract in a separate bowl. Pour the wet ingredients into the dry ingredients and stir until just combined.

Heat a non-stick skillet over medium heat. Pour 1/4 cup of batter onto the skillet for each pancake. Cook until bubbles form on the surface, then flip and cook until golden brown. Repeat with the remaining batter.

Mixed Berry Compote Recipe

While your pancakes are cooking, you can prepare the mixed berry compote. This compote is like the crown jewel on your stack of pancakes, adding a burst of fruity sweetness.

- 2 cups mixed berries (fresh or frozen)
- 2 tablespoons maple syrup
- 1 teaspoon lemon juice

Combine the berries and maple syrup in a saucepan. Cook over medium heat until the berries break down, and the mixture thickens about 10-15 minutes. Remove from heat and stir in the lemon juice.

Serving Suggestions

It's time for the grand finale: serving your breakfast

masterpiece. Stack your warm, fluffy pancakes on a plate. Pour the glossy berry compote over the top, letting it seep into every nook and cranny. You might want to add a dollop of plant-based yogurt for extra creaminess or a sprinkle of chia seeds for a crunchy contrast. And there you have it: a breakfast that's nourishing and satisfying and a feast for the eyes.

Remember, breakfast is more than just the first meal of the day. It's an opportunity to nourish your body, awaken your senses, and set a positive tone for the rest of your day. So, savor the quiet moments of the morning, the simple act of preparing your food, and the first delicious bite of your day. Here's to a day as marvelous and vibrant as your breakfast.

### 5.2 Scrambled Tofu Breakfast Tacos

*(Serves 4-6 people, 150-200 calories/serving, one taco. Tofu is a plant-based source of protein and provides essential amino acids. It is also a good source of iron, calcium, and other minerals).*

### Tofu Scramble Ingredients

Let's kick things off with the star of our breakfast tacos - the scrambled tofu. This protein-packed filling is incredibly delicious and easy to whip up. Here's what you'll need:

- 1 block (14 ounces) of firm tofu
- 2 tablespoons nutritional yeast
- 1/2 teaspoon turmeric
- 1/2 teaspoon garlic powder
- Salt and pepper to taste
- A splash of plant-based milk
- 1 tablespoon olive oil
- 1 small onion, diced
- 1 bell pepper, diced

First, drain and press the tofu to remove as much liquid as possible. This will help achieve a scrambled egg-like texture. Next, crumble the tofu into a bowl and add the nutritional yeast, turmeric, garlic powder, salt, pepper, and a splash of plant-based milk. Stir well to combine.

Heat the olive oil in a pan over medium heat. Add the diced onion and bell pepper, and sauté until they soften. Add the tofu mixture and cook, stirring occasionally, until everything is heated and the flavors melded together.

### Taco Assembly Instructions

With your scrambled tofu ready, it's time to assemble your breakfast tacos. For this, you'll need:

- Small corn or whole wheat tortillas
- The scrambled tofu
- Your choice of fillings (see optional toppings below)

Warm the tortillas in a dry pan over medium heat until they're soft and pliable. Spoon a generous helping of the scrambled tofu onto each tortilla. Now, add your toppings and bring these breakfast tacos to life.

Optional Toppings

Toppings are the fun part, where you can let your imagination run wild. They add color, texture, and even more flavor to your breakfast tacos. Here are a few ideas:

- Sliced avocado or a spoonful of guacamole adds creaminess and a dose of healthy fats.
- A sprinkle of chopped fresh cilantro brings a pop of green and freshness.
- A spoonful of salsa or a drizzle of hot sauce lends a bit of heat and flavor.
- A squeeze of fresh lime juice adds a bright, zesty note that combines all the flavors.

And voila, you've created a breakfast that's as vibrant and energizing as your day ahead. As you savor each bite, let the flavors dance on your palate, the textures delight your senses, and the nutrients fuel your body. This is the beauty of plant-based eating - every meal and bite is an opportunity to nourish yourself with the bountiful goodness of whole plant foods. So, enjoy your scrambled tofu breakfast tacos, and here's to a day filled with health, vitality, and delicious plant-based eats.

### 5.3 OVERNIGHT CHIA PUDDING VARIATIONS

*(Serves 1, 200-250 cal/serving; Chia seeds are a superfood known for their nutritional value. They are an excellent source of fiber, omega-3 fatty acids, antioxidants, and various vitamins and minerals).*

#### Basic Chia Pudding Recipe

Imagine waking up to a breakfast that's already prepared, waiting for you in the refrigerator — a breakfast that's not only delicious but also packed with nutrients. That's the magic of overnight chia pudding. This no-cook, make-ahead breakfast is a game-changer for busy mornings. Here's how to make the basic version:

- 1/4 cup chia seeds
- 1 cup plant-based milk
- 1 tablespoon maple syrup

Combine the chia seeds, plant-based milk, and maple syrup in a mason jar or a bowl. Stir well to ensure no clumps of chia seeds remain. Cover and refrigerate overnight. By morning, the chia seeds will have soaked up the liquid, turning into a pudding-like consistency.

Chocolate Banana Variation

Add a touch of indulgence to your morning with this chocolate banana variation of chia pudding. It's like having dessert for breakfast but with the benefit of being nutritious.

- Basic chia pudding recipe
- 1 tablespoon cocoa powder
- 1 ripe banana, mashed

While preparing the basic chia pudding, add the cocoa powder and mashed banana to the mix. Stir well to combine, ensuring there are no lumps of cocoa powder. Cover and refrigerate overnight. In the morning, you'll be greeted with a rich, chocolatey pudding naturally sweetened with banana.

Mixed Berry Variation

Try this mixed berry variation for a refreshing, fruity twist on your chia pudding. It's like a taste of summer, no matter what time of the year.

- Basic chia pudding recipe
- 1 cup mixed berries (fresh or frozen)
- Optional: extra berries for topping

While preparing the basic chia pudding, add the mixed berries. If you're using fresh berries, you can mash them slightly with a fork to release their juices. If you're using frozen berries, they will thaw overnight and infuse the pudding with their fruity flavor. Cover and refrigerate overnight. In the morning, top with extra berries for a burst of freshness.

<u>Tropical Fruit Variation</u>

Transport yourself to a tropical paradise with this tropical fruit variation of chia pudding. It's a great way to start your day on a bright, cheerful note.

- Basic chia pudding recipe
- 1/2 cup diced mango (fresh or frozen)
- 1/2 cup diced pineapple (fresh or frozen)
- Optional: toasted coconut flakes for topping

While preparing the basic chia pudding, add the diced mango and pineapple. If you're using fresh fruit, you can add it directly to the mix. If you're using frozen fruit, it will thaw overnight and give the pudding a tropical twist. Cover and refrigerate overnight. In the morning, sprinkle with toasted coconut flakes for a bit of crunch.

With these overnight chia pudding variations, your breakfasts will never be boring again. Whether you're craving something indulgent like the chocolate banana pudding, something refreshing like the mixed berry pudding, or something exotic like the tropical fruit pudding, there's a chia pudding for every taste. And the best part? They're all packed with nutrients to fuel your day. So, try these recipes and enjoy the convenience and versatility of overnight chia pudding. Who knew that breakfast could be so easy, delicious, and nutritious?

### **5.4 GREEN SMOOTHIE BOWLS**

*(One Serving, 250-350 cal/serving. Fresh spinach is a nutritious leafy green rich in vitamins, particularly vitamins K, A, and folate. It also provides essential minerals like iron and calcium).*

<u>Base Green Smoothie Recipe</u>

Let's stage our green smoothie bowl with a basic yet flavorful recipe. This smoothie base blends healthful ingredients that balance essential nutrients to kick-start your morning. Here's what you'll need:

- 1 ripe banana, frozen
- 1/2 cup fresh spinach
- 1/2 cup plant-based milk
- 1 tablespoon chia seeds
- 1 tablespoon nut butter

Place the frozen banana, fresh spinach, plant-based milk,

chia seeds, and nut butter into your blender. Blend on high until the mixture is smooth and creamy. The frozen banana offers natural sweetness and a creamy texture, while the spinach adds a vibrant green color and a dose of leafy greens to your breakfast. On the other hand, Chia seeds and nut butter provide a healthy dose of fats and protein, ensuring your smoothie bowl is as nourishing as it is tasty.

<u>Topping Ideas</u>

With the canvas of your smoothie bowl laid out, it's time to add some creative flair to your toppings. Toppings add visual appeal, a range of textures, and additional nutrients. Here are some topping ideas:

- Fresh fruits: Berries, sliced bananas, or kiwi add a pop of color and boost vitamins.
- Nuts and seeds: Almonds, walnuts, or sunflower seeds add a satisfying crunch and a dose of healthy fats.
- Granola or muesli: For an added crunch and a hint of sweetness, sprinkle a handful of your favorite granola or muesli.
- Nut butter: A drizzle of almond, cashew, or peanut butter can add a rich, creamy element and extra protein.

Remember, when it comes to toppings, the sky's the limit! Feel free to customize based on your preferences and what you have on hand.

<u>Presentation Tips</u>

One of the joys of a smoothie bowl is its visual appeal. The vibrant colors, the array of textures, the artful arrangement of toppings - it's like a feast for the eyes. Here are a few tips to enhance the presentation of your smoothie bowl:

- Choose a bowl that complements your smoothie's color. A contrasting color can make your smoothie bowl pop.
- Arrange your toppings in an aesthetically pleasing way. You could create rows of different toppings, arrange them in a circular pattern, or scatter them on top.
- Think about color. Use a variety of colored fruits, nuts, and seeds to make your smoothie bowl vibrant and eye-catching.
- Don't overfill your bowl. Leave some space for the smoothie to peek through, showcasing the beautiful green color.

A green smoothie bowl is a delightful way to start your day. It's like a symphony of flavors and textures in every spoonful - the creaminess of the smoothie, the crunch of the toppings, the sweetness of the fruit, the richness of the nut butter. It's a breakfast that's as pleasing to the eye as it is to the palate, as nourishing for the body as it is for the soul. So, grab your spoon and savor the goodness of plant-based breakfasts. It's a morning ritual that celebrates the joy of eating, the beauty of whole foods, and the pleasure of caring for your health.

As we wrap up this chapter, remember that each meal is an opportunity to nourish your body, tantalize your taste buds, and express your creativity. Whether it's a stack of whole grain pancakes, a plate of tofu scramble tacos, or a vibrant green smoothie bowl, there's a world of delicious, nutritious breakfasts waiting for you in the plant-based cuisine. So, prepare to greet the day with a satisfied stomach and a heart full of joy. We're moving on to the next delicious meal of the day. Stay tuned!

# CHAPTER 6

## MIDDAY MARVELS: PLANT-BASED LUNCHES FOR ENERGY AND SATISFACTION

Imagine the sun at its zenith, casting warm, radiant light on a day full of potential. You've navigated the morning with grace and vigor; now, it's time to refuel. Lunch is more than just a break in your day. It's an opportunity to energize your body, stimulate your senses, and keep your productivity levels high for the rest of the day. Welcome to the world of plant-based lunches, where nutrition, flavor, and creativity come together in perfect harmony.

The beauty of plant-based lunches lies in their versatility. Whether at home, at work, or on the go, a plant-based lunch is just right for you. So, let's roll up our sleeves and start with a dish that's as vibrant as it is nourishing - a quinoa salad with roasted vegetables.

### 6.1 Quinoa Salad with Roasted Veggies

*(Serves 4-6 people, 200-250 cal/serving, one bowl. Quinoa is a nutritious grain that is a good source of protein, dietary fiber, and various vitamins and minerals, including magnesium and iron).*

### Quinoa Cooking Instructions

Quinoa, a nutrient-dense whole grain, forms the hearty base of our salad. It's packed with plant-based protein and fiber, making it a satisfying and nutritious choice.

To cook quinoa, rinse 1 cup of quinoa under cold water to remove any bitter saponins. Place the rinsed quinoa in a saucepan and add 2 cups of water. Bring the mixture to a boil, then reduce the heat, cover the pot, and let it simmer for about 15 minutes, or until the quinoa has absorbed all the water and is tender. Remove from heat and let it sit, covered, for 5 minutes to fluff up.

Roasted Vegetable Selection

While your quinoa is cooking, you can prepare your roasted veggies. Roasting vegetables brings out their natural sweetness and gives them a delightful, caramelized flavor. For this salad, choose a variety of colorful veggies for a vibrant and nutrient-rich dish. Some good options are bell peppers, zucchini, cherry tomatoes, and red onions.

Cut your veggies into bite-sized pieces, toss them in olive oil, and spread them out on a baking sheet. Roast them in a 425°F (220°C) oven for about 20-25 minutes or until tender and slightly charred.

Salad Dressing Recipe

A salad isn't complete without a delicious dressing, and for this quinoa salad, we'll whip up a simple lemon-tahini dressing. Tahini, a paste made from sesame seeds, gives the dressing a creamy texture and a nutty flavor, while lemon juice adds a freshness.

- 1/4 cup of tahini
- juice of 1 lemon
- 2 tablespoons of olive oil
- 1-2 tablespoons of water

To make the dressing, whisk together the tahini, lemon juice, and olive oil, and add 1-2 tablespoons of water to thin it out. Season it with salt and pepper to taste.

Combine the cooked quinoa, roasted veggies, and dressing to assemble your salad in a large bowl. Toss until everything is well coated with the dressing. You can enjoy the salad as it is or add some extras like fresh herbs, toasted nuts, or even some diced avocado for creaminess. This quinoa salad is a testament to the power of plant-based foods, where simple ingredients come together to create a symphony of flavors and a powerhouse of nutrition. It's a midday meal that energizes and satisfies until dinner.

The beauty of plant-based lunches lies in their versatility. Whether at home, at work, or on the go, a plant-based lunch is just right for you. So, let's roll up our sleeves and start with a dish that's as vibrant as it is nourishing - a quinoa salad with roasted vegetables.

### 6.2 Spicy Lentil Wraps with Tahini Sauce

*(Serves 1-2 people, 400-500 calories/serving, one wrap. Lentils are a nutritious source of plant-based protein, fiber, and essential vitamins and minerals. They are also low in fat and can help maintain a healthy weight).*

#### Spicy Lentil Preparation

Lentils, these tiny legumes, are about to take center stage

in your kitchen as the star filling for your wraps. We will turn up the heat a notch by adding spice to this protein-packed powerhouse.

- 1 cup of dried lentils
- 3 cups of water
- 1 teaspoon ground cumin
- 1 teaspoon ground coriander
- 1 teaspoon smoked paprika
- 1/2 teaspoon of turmeric
- 1/4 teaspoon of cayenne pepper

To begin, post-cooking, you will need one cup of dried lentils, preferably green or brown, for their firm texture. Rinse them under cold water and place them in a pot with three cups of water. Bring the water to a boil, reduce the heat, cover the pot, and let it simmer.

The lentils will need about 20-25 minutes to cook to a tender yet firm consistency. While the lentils are simmering, you can prepare the spice mix. Combine a teaspoon of ground cumin, ground coriander, smoked paprika, half a teaspoon of turmeric, and a quarter teaspoon of cayenne pepper. Feel free to adjust the spices according to your taste, especially the cayenne pepper, if you prefer a milder flavor.

Once the lentils are cooked, drain any excess water and return the lentils to the pot. Stir in the spice mix, ensuring the lentils are evenly coated. Set aside the spiced lentils to cool slightly while you prepare the tahini sauce.

Tahini Sauce Recipe

This creamy tahini sauce will bring a rich and tangy element to your wraps, complementing the spicy lentils perfectly. In a bowl, combine a quarter cup of tahini, a paste made from sesame seeds, with the juice of one lemon. Stir in a minced garlic clove for a hint of sharpness, and season with salt. The sauce might be a bit thick, so stir in warm water, a tablespoon at a time, until it reaches a pourable consistency.

<u>Wrap Assembly Instructions</u>

Now comes the fun part — assembling the wraps. You will need large tortillas that can hold the fillings without tearing. Whole wheat tortillas are an excellent choice for their added nutritional value.

Warm the tortillas slightly to make them more pliable. You can do this by heating them in a dry skillet over medium heat on each side for 30 seconds. Lay out a tortilla and spread a generous spoonful of the tahini sauce in the center. Top this with a few spoonfuls of the spicy lentils.

At this point, you can add any additional fillings you like. Some thinly sliced cucumber or bell pepper will add a nice crunch, a handful of fresh spinach or lettuce will bring a touch of freshness, and some sliced avocado will contribute a creamy richness. Just be careful not to overfill the wrap, making it hard to roll.

To roll the wrap, fold in the sides over the fillings, then roll up from the bottom. Repeat with the remaining tortillas and fillings. Slice the wraps in half on the diagonal, revealing the colorful layers of filling inside.

There you have it, a delicious and nutritious plant-based lunch packed with flavor and portable enough to take on the go. Spicy lentil wraps with tahini sauce — a simple yet satisfying meal that will spice up your lunch routine. Enjoy!

## 6.3 HEARTY MINESTRONE SOUP

*(Serves 4-6 people, 150-200 cal/serving, one bowl. Minestrone is packed with vegetables, a good source of vitamins and minerals like vitamin C, vitamin A, potassium, and dietary fiber. These nutrients support overall health and immune function).*

SOUP BASE RECIPE

Minestrone, a classic Italian dish, is like a warm hug in a bowl. It's a rainbow medley of vegetables simmered in a flavorful broth and rounded off with hearty grains or pasta. Let's start with the foundation of our soup - the base.

- 2 tablespoons of olive oil
- 1 diced onion
- 2 diced carrots
- 2 diced celery stalks
- 3 garlic cloves, minced
- 6 cups of vegetable broth
- One 14-ounce can of diced tomatoes.
- Salt, pepper & bay leaves

In a large pot, heat the olive oil over medium heat. Add the onion, diced carrots, and diced celery stalks, cooking until the vegetables soften and the onion becomes translucent. Add the minced garlic cloves, cooking for another minute until fragrant.

Now, pour in the vegetable broth, bringing a savory depth to your soup. Add the can of diced tomatoes, with their juice, for a bit of tanginess and body—season with salt, pepper, and a couple of bay leaves for an earthy note.

Bring the soup to a boil, then reduce the heat to low and let it simmer. This soup base is like a blank canvas, ready to be adorned with various vegetables, grains, and legumes.

Vegetable Selection

Selecting the vegetables for your minestrone is like arranging a bouquet. You want a variety of colors, textures, and flavors. Traditional minestrone often includes zucchini, green beans, and spinach. But feel free to use whatever vegetables you have on hand or prefer.

If you're using zucchini and green beans, add them to the pot after the soup has been simmering for about 10 minutes. They'll need another 10-15 minutes to cook until tender.

For the spinach, wait until the last few minutes of cooking time. It wilts quickly and retains a vibrant color when not overcooked.

<u>Serving Suggestions</u>

As you ladle your hearty minestrone into bowls, consider what accompaniments might enhance this wholesome meal. A freshly grated vegan Parmesan sprinkle can add a salty, cheesy note. A piece of crusty whole-grain bread on the side is perfect for soaking up the flavorful broth.

If you'd like to add some grains to your soup, cooked quinoa or whole-grain pasta are great additions. Remember to cook them separately and add them to each serving to prevent them from becoming mushy.

Your hearty minestrone is now ready to be savored. Each spoonful celebrates plant-based goodness, a symphony of flavors and textures. It's a testament to the beauty of simplicity and the power of plant-based ingredients. So, sit back, warm up with a bowl of minestrone, and let the comfort of this classic dish wash over you.

### 6.4 <u>Veggie Sushi Rolls</u>

*(Serves 4-6 people, 150-200 cal/roll. Sushi rice, seasoned with rice vinegar, sugar, and salt, provides carbohydrates as an energy source. It's also gluten-free and low in fat).*

## Sushi Rice Preparation

Let's turn our attention to the heart of the sushi roll - the rice. The marriage between the slightly vinegary, sticky rice and the delicate flavors of the vegetables is what makes sushi such a delight. Here's what you'll need;

- 2 cups of uncooked sushi rice
- 2 cups of water
- 1/3 cup of rice vinegar
- 2 tablespoons of sugar
- 1 teaspoon of salt

To begin with, you'll need sushi rice, a short-grain Japanese rice known for its sticky texture when cooked. We'll need about 2 cups of uncooked sushi rice for our sushi rolls.

Start by rinsing the rice under cold water until the water runs clear. This helps to remove the excess starch and prevents the rice from becoming too gummy when cooked. After rinsing, place the rice in a saucepan with 2 cups of water. Please bring it to a boil, then cover the pot, reduce the heat to low, and let it simmer for about 20 minutes, or until the water is absorbed and the rice is tender.

While the rice is cooking, prepare the vinegar mixture that will season the rice. Combine 1/3 cup of rice vinegar, two tablespoons of sugar, and one teaspoon of salt in a small saucepan. Heat gently and stir until the sugar and salt dissolve.

Once the rice is cooked, transfer it to a large wooden or glass bowl (avoid metal as it can react with the vinegar). Drizzle over the vinegar mixture while the rice is still hot, and gently fold it into the rice using a wooden spatula. It's important to be gentle during this process to avoid crushing rice grains. Let the rice cool to room temperature before making sushi rolls.

<u>Vegetable Filling Options</u>

While the sushi rice is the show's star, the vegetable fillings are the vibrant supporting cast. They add color, texture, and a variety of flavors to each bite.

Consider contrasting colors and textures when choosing the vegetables for your sushi rolls. Some good options include cucumber for a refreshing crunch, avocado for creaminess, carrot for a sweet note, and bell pepper for a pop of color.

Start by cutting your chosen vegetables into thin strips. The size of the strips will depend on the size of your nori sheets and how much filling you prefer in your sushi rolls.

<u>Rolling Technique</u>

Rolling sushi is a skill that might take a little practice, but once you get the hang of it, it's pretty straightforward. You'll need a bamboo sushi mat, which helps to shape and tighten the roll.

Start by laying a sheet of nori on the sushi mat. Wet your hands and grab a handful of the cooled sushi rice. Spread it evenly over the nori, leaving about an inch free at the top. Press the rice down firmly but gently.

Arrange your vegetable strips in a line on the rice, about a third up from the bottom of the nori. Now, it's time to roll. Start rolling from the bottom using the sushi mat and tucking in the vegetables. Keep rolling until you reach the top, then use a bit of water to seal the edge of the nori.

Use a sharp knife to cut the roll into bite-sized pieces. And there you have it, your very own homemade veggie sushi rolls!

And so, with a delicious array of plant-based lunches at your fingertips, you're well-equipped to navigate the midday meal with flair and creativity. Each recipe, each dish, is a testament to the vibrant diversity of plant-based eating, a celebration of the bounty of whole foods. The symphony of flavors, the rainbow of colors, the array of textures - they all come together to create meals that nourish your body and delight your senses. So, please take a moment to savor your creations, appreciate the beauty of plant-based foods, and honor the nourishment they provide. After all, it's not just about eating; it's about celebrating food, health, and life. Now, let's continue our culinary adventure as we explore the next meal of the day. Onward to the world of plant-based dinners!

**Powering the Plant-Based Future**

"The gods created certain kinds of beings to replenish our

bodies; they are the trees and the plants and the seeds." — Plato

A survey of 30,000 people across the world conducted by GlobeScan and EAT found that 42% of respondents thought that "most people will definitely or probably" be eating plant-based food in place of animal products in the next decade. That's a huge percentage, and it shows the desire many of us have to move toward a more plant-based

lifestyle.

Yet for many people, the idea is very intimidating. Information is contradictory, and there's so much to learn – especially if you're someone who grew up with meat, eggs, and cheese being staple parts of your diet. What people need is confidence, and it's my aim with this book to inspire it. There's a whole world of plant-based adventures ahead of you after you close this book: This is the foundation you can build on.

My goal was to make plant-based eating as accessible as possible and provide clear, uncomplicated guidance on how to pursue it… and now I'd like to ask for your help in reaching more of the people who believe that this lifestyle is the way forward but don't know how to get started themselves. The good news is, that's only going to take a few minutes of your time, but it's going to have a huge impact.

**By leaving a review of this book on Amazon, you'll not only show readers who are looking for this guidance where to find it; you'll show them that plant-based eating really isn't as intimidating as they fear.**

There are so many people looking for this information,

and as someone who already sees how important it is for us to move toward a healthier and more sustainable way of living, you're the perfect person to help them find it.

Thank you so much for your support. Together, we can empower more people to make the changes they've been longing to make for a long time.

# CHAPTER 7

## DELICIOUSLY SATISFYING: PLANT-BASED DINNERS TO WRAP UP YOUR DAY

The sun dips below the horizon, painting the sky with hues of orange and pink. The day's work is done; now it's time to unwind. It is a time to gather around the dinner table, share stories of the day, and nourish our bodies with a hearty, plant-based meal. With the right ingredients and techniques, creating a satisfying plant-based dinner is easier than you might think. Let's dive into the first recipe of this chapter - a comforting chickpea curry served with fluffy basmati rice.

### 7.1 CHICKPEA CURRY WITH BASMATI RICE

*(Serves four people, 300-350 cal/serving, one bowl. Chickpeas are a good source of plant-based protein and dietary fiber. They also provide essential nutrients like folate, iron, and manganese).*

### Chickpea Curry Recipe

Think of chickpeas as a reliable friend who always has your back. Chickpeas are a staple in plant-based cuisine and are high in protein, fiber, and a range of vital nutrients. In this recipe, they're simmered in a flavorful curry sauce, creating a dish that's as comforting as it is nutritious.

You'll need:

- 1 can (14 ounces) of chickpeas, drained and rinsed
- 1 large onion, diced
- 3 cloves of garlic, minced
- 1 tablespoon of fresh ginger, grated
- 1 can (14 ounces) of diced tomatoes
- 1 can (14 ounces) of coconut milk
- 2 tablespoons of curry powder
- 1 teaspoon of turmeric
- 1 teaspoon of cumin
- Salt to taste
- 2 tablespoons of olive oil
- Fresh cilantro for garnish

Start by heating the olive oil in a large pot over medium

heat. Add the diced onion and cook until it begins to soften. Stir in the minced garlic and grated ginger, cooking for another minute until fragrant. Add the curry powder, turmeric, and cumin, stirring well to coat the onions with the spices.

Next, add the diced tomatoes, juice, and coconut milk to the pot. Stir in the drained chickpeas. Bring the mixture to a boil, then reduce the heat and let it simmer for about 20 minutes. This allows the flavors to meld together and the chickpeas to absorb the aromatic curry sauce—season with salt to taste.

<u>Basmati Rice Cooking Instructions</u>

You can prepare the basmati rice while your chickpea curry is simmering away. Known for its aromatic fragrance and delicate flavor, basmati rice perfectly accompanies the robust curry.

You'll need:

- 1 cup of basmati rice
- 2 cups of water
- A pinch of salt

Rinse the basmati rice under cold water until the water runs clear. This removes the excess starch and helps the rice cook up fluffy and separate. Place the rinsed rice in a pot with the water and a pinch of salt. Please bring it to a boil, cover the pot, reduce the heat to low, and let it simmer for about 15 minutes until all the water is absorbed and the rice is tender.

<u>Serving Suggestions</u>

To serve your chickpea curry and basmati rice, spoon a generous helping of rice onto one side of a plate or a shallow bowl. Spoon the chickpea curry next to the rice. Garnish with fresh cilantro for a pop of color and freshness.

As you taste this comforting chickpea curry with basmati rice, notice how the curry flavors meld together, creating a symphony of taste in your mouth. The firmness of the chickpeas, the creaminess of the curry sauce, the delicate fluffiness of the rice - a harmony of textures that adds to the overall enjoyment of the meal.

This chickpea curry with basmati rice is more than just a dinner. It's a celebration of the simplicity and variety of plant-based foods. It's a testament that humble, plant-based ingredients can create nourishing, flavorful meals. So, savor this meal, share it with loved ones, and take pleasure in the fact that you're nourishing your body with the goodness of whole plant foods. And remember, this is just the beginning of your plant-based dinner adventures. There are many more delicious recipes and techniques to explore, each a new opportunity to celebrate the joy of plant-based eating.

## 7.2 STUFFED BELL PEPPERS

*(Serves four people, 300-350 cal/serving, one stuffed bell pepper. Quinoa is a nutrient-rich whole grain that is a good source of protein and dietary fiber. It's also rich in vitamins and minerals, including manganese, magnesium, and phosphorus).*

Bell Pepper Selection

Picking out the perfect bell peppers for your stuffed creation is akin to choosing the perfect apple for your pie. You're looking for firmness, vibrant color, and an excellent round shape that can stand upright in your baking dish. Bell peppers come in various colors, each with its unique flavor profile. The green ones are slightly bitter, the red ones are sweet, and the yellow and orange ones are somewhere in between. Any color will work for this recipe, so select the ones most appealing to you.

Stuffing Recipe

With your bell peppers chosen, it's time to create the stuffing to transform them into a hearty, satisfying meal. We'll use a combination of quinoa, black beans, corn, and spices. You'll need;

- 1 cup of quinoa
- 1 tablespoon of olive oil
- 1 diced onion
- 2 cloves of garlic, minced
- 1 cup of cooked black beans
- 1 cup of corn kernels (fresh, frozen, or canned)
- 1 teaspoon of chili powder
- 1/2 teaspoon of cumin
- Salt to taste

Begin by cooking the quinoa according to the package instructions. Quinoa is an excellent source of plant-based protein and adds a delightful, nutty flavor to the stuffing.

While the quinoa is cooking, heat the olive oil in a pan and sauté the diced onion until it becomes translucent. Stir in the minced garlic and cook for another minute until the garlic is fragrant.

Next, add the cooked black beans and corn kernels (fresh, frozen, or canned) to the pan. Black beans add protein and a satisfying meaty texture, while corn offers sweetness and crunch.

Season the mixture with the chili powder, cumin, and salt to taste. These spices will add warmth and depth to the stuffing.

Finally, stir in the cooked quinoa until everything is well combined. Your stuffing is now ready to be nestled into the bell peppers.

<u>Baking Instructions</u>

Preheat your oven to 375°F (190°C) and prepare a baking dish by lightly greasing it with a bit of olive oil.

Cut off the tops of your bell peppers and scoop out the seeds and membranes. Fill each pepper with the quinoa and bean stuffing, pressing down slightly to ensure they're well packed.

Place the stuffed peppers upright in the baking dish. Cover the dish with foil and bake for about 30 minutes. After 30 minutes, remove the foil and continue baking for another 15-20 minutes, or until the peppers are tender and the stuffing is heated.

There you have it: a plant-based dinner that is filling, nutritious, and brimming with flavor. As you savor your stuffed bell pepper, take a moment to appreciate how simple ingredients have come together to create such a delightful dish. Each bite is a testament to the versatility and deliciousness of plant-based foods. So, embrace the process, enjoy the flavors, and remember, every meal is a chance to nourish your body and delight your taste buds. Let's continue to explore more plant-based dinner creations in the following recipe.

### 7.3 Sweet Potato Gnocchi

*(Serves four people, 180-240 cal/serving, 8-10 gnocchi. Sweet potatoes are rich in vitamins and minerals, including vitamins A, C, and potassium. They are also a good source of dietary fiber, making them a nutritious addition to the recipe).*

### Gnocchi Dough Recipe

Envision the humble sweet potato, a vibrant tuber packed with nutrients and natural sweetness. Now, picture it transformed into tender, plump gnocchi, ready to be enveloped in your favorite sauce. To make sweet potato gnocchi, you'll need:

- 2 medium sweet potatoes
- 1 1/2 - 2 cups of whole wheat or all-purpose flour
- 1/2 teaspoon of salt

Start by baking the sweet potatoes in a 400°F (200°C) oven for about 45 minutes or until tender. Once they're cool enough to handle, peel them and mash the flesh until smooth.

Add the salt, and add the flour, a bit at a time, until a soft dough forms. You might not need all the flour, or you might need a bit more. The goal is a dough firm enough to hold its shape yet still soft to the touch.

### Cooking Instructions

Once your dough is ready, it's time to shape it into gnocchi. Divide the dough into four equal pieces. Roll each piece into a long rope, about 1 inch in diameter. Slice each rope into 1-inch pieces.

To give your gnocchi the traditional ridged shape, you can press each piece against the tines of a fork, rolling it slightly. This isn't just for appearance - these ridges will help your gnocchi hold more sauce.

Bring a large pot of salted water to a boil to cook your gnocchi. Add the gnocchi and cook until they float to the surface, which should take 2-3 minutes. Once they're floating, let them cook for another minute, then drain.

<u>Sauce Pairings</u>

Now that your sweet potato gnocchi are cooked, you might wonder what sauce to pair them with. The beauty of gnocchi is their versatility - they're a perfect canvas for various sauces.

For a simple yet flavorful option, consider a sage brown butter sauce. Melt some vegan butter in a pan, let it brown slightly, then add fresh sage leaves. The butter will turn nutty and aromatic, and the sage leaves crispy. Toss your cooked gnocchi in this sauce for an elegant yet easy dish.

If you want something creamy, a vegan Alfredo sauce could be just the ticket. Made with cashews and nutritional yeast, this sauce is rich, creamy, and perfect for coating your sweet potato gnocchi.

Or, for a burst of freshness, try a basil pesto sauce. Made with fresh basil, garlic, pine nuts, and olive oil, it's a vibrant sauce that pairs beautifully with the sweetness of the gnocchi.

So there you have it, sweet potato gnocchi, a plant-based dinner that's as delightful to prepare as it is to eat. Each pillowy morsel is a little bite of comfort, a testament to the transformative power of plant-based ingredients. Whether dining alone or sharing with loved ones, this meal will bring warmth to your dinner table.

### 7.4 Mushroom and Spinach Risotto

*(Serves four people, 350-400 cal/serving, one medium bowl. Arborio rice is a starchy short-grain rice variety used in risotto. It provides carbohydrates and is a source of energy).*

Risotto Base Recipe

Transport your palate to the heart of Italy with this sumptuous mushroom and spinach risotto. Risotto, a creamy rice dish hailing from Northern Italy, is an authentic comfort food, marrying simple ingredients into a rich and satisfying dish.

Arborio rice is the foundation of any risotto, a short-grain rice known for its high starch content, which lends the dish its characteristic creaminess. To start, you'll need:

- 1 cup of Arborio rice
- 1 small onion, finely chopped
- 2 cloves of garlic, minced
- 4 cups of vegetable broth
- 1/2 cup of white wine
- 2 tablespoons of olive oil
- Salt to taste

Heat the olive oil in a large, deep skillet or a Dutch oven over medium heat. Add the chopped onion and cook until it becomes translucent. Stir in the minced garlic and continue to cook until fragrant. Add the Arborio rice to the skillet, stirring well to coat the grains with the oil.

Pour in the white wine and let it simmer until the liquid evaporates. Add the vegetable broth, one ladle at a time, stirring frequently. Wait until each ladle of broth is almost fully absorbed before adding the next. Adding broth releases the rice's starch, creating a creamy, velvety risotto.

Mushroom and Spinach Addition

With your risotto base coming along nicely, it's time to introduce the stars of the show: earthy mushrooms and vibrant spinach. For this, you'll need:

- 2 cups of sliced mushrooms
- 2 cups of fresh spinach
- 1 tablespoon of olive oil

- Salt and pepper to taste

In a separate skillet, heat the olive oil over medium heat. Add the sliced mushrooms, cooking until they're tender and lightly browned—season with salt and pepper to taste. Stir in the fresh spinach and cook until it's just wilted.

<u>Serving Suggestions</u>

Once your risotto is creamy and the rice is al dente, gently fold in the cooked mushrooms and spinach. Allow the risotto to rest for a few minutes before serving. This allows all the flavors and the risotto to achieve the perfect creamy consistency.

To serve, spoon a generous helping of the mushroom and spinach risotto into a bowl. If you'd like, garnish with a sprinkle of nutritional yeast for a cheesy flavor or a handful of fresh herbs for an added pop of color and freshness.

In creating this risotto, you've seen how simple, plant-based ingredients can come together to form a meal that's both nourishing and profoundly satisfying. Each spoonful of the creamy Arborio rice, each bite of the earthy mushrooms, each taste of the vibrant spinach - a mixture of flavors and textures that's genuinely a pleasure to eat. So, take a moment to savor this meal, appreciate the art of plant-based cooking, and delight in the knowledge that you're fueling your body with the best nature has to offer.

As we close this chapter, remember that plant-based dinners are more than just meals. They're an opportunity to explore new ingredients, experiment with different cooking techniques, and create dishes that are as pleasing to the palate as they are beneficial to your health. So, whether you're enjoying a hearty chickpea curry, a vibrant stuffed bell pepper, or a creamy mushroom and spinach risotto, know that each bite is a testament to the power and deliciousness of plant-based foods. The adventure doesn't end here, though - there's still a world of plant-based meals to explore, and we're just getting started.

# CHAPTER 8

## NOURISHING BITES: PLANT-BASED SNACKS AND SIDES

Whoever said that good things come in small packages must have been thinking about snacks. These miniature meals are more than just a way to overcome hunger between larger meals. They're an opportunity to infuse your day with bursts of energy, flavor, and nutrition. Similarly, side dishes can elevate a meal from good to great, adding diversity in flavors and textures. This chapter will explore the world of plant-based snacks and sides, starting with a timeless favorite - hummus.

### 8.1 Classic Hummus

*(Serves six people, 70-9- cal/serving, small cup. Chickpeas, or garbanzo beans, are the primary ingredient in hummus. They are an excellent source of plant-based protein, fiber, and various vitamins and minerals).*

Hummus, a creamy spread made from chickpeas, is a staple in Middle Eastern cuisine and has gained global popularity due to its versatility and health benefits. It's rich in plant-based protein, fiber, and heart-healthy fats. Plus, it's effortless to make at home.

<u>Hummus Ingredients</u>

To make your classic hummus, you'll need:

- 1 can (15 ounces) of chickpeas, drained and rinsed
- 1/4 cup fresh lemon juice (about 1 large lemon)
- 1/4 cup well-stirred tahini
- 1 small garlic clove, minced
- 2 tablespoons extra virgin olive oil, plus more for serving

- 1/2 teaspoon ground cumin
- Salt to taste
- 2 to 3 tablespoons water
- Dash of ground paprika for serving

<u>Blending Instructions</u>

Start by combining tahini and lemon juice in a food processor and process for about 1 minute. This extra step helps to 'cream' or 'whip' the tahini, making the hummus smooth and creamy.

Add olive oil, minced garlic, cumin, and a 1/2 teaspoon of salt to the whipped tahini and lemon juice. Process for about 30 seconds, scrape the sides and bottom of the bowl, then process another 30 seconds.

Add half of the chickpeas to the food processor and process for 1 minute. Add chickpeas and process until thick and relatively smooth; 1 to 2 minutes. If the hummus is too thick or still has tiny bits of chickpea, with the food processor turned on, slowly add 2 to 3 tablespoons of water until you reach the perfect consistency.

<u>Serving Ideas</u>

Hummus is incredibly versatile and can be served in a variety of ways. You could spread it on a slice of whole-grain toast for a quick and nutritious snack. It makes an excellent dip for cut-up vegetables like cucumber sticks, carrot sticks, or cherry tomatoes. Add a dollop to your salad for some extra creaminess and flavor. It's also delicious in wraps or sandwiches, adding a layer of moisture and richness.

To serve hummus as a snack or appetizer, scoop it into a bowl, drizzle it with olive oil, and sprinkle it with a dash of paprika for color and a hint of smoky flavor. You could also top it with whole chickpeas or fresh herbs for extra visual appeal.

So there you have it, a delicious and nutritious snack or side that takes mere minutes to prepare. With its creamy texture, rich flavor, and nutrient-packed profile, classic hummus will surely become a favorite in your plant-based repertoire. Just remember, when it comes to plant-based snacks and sides, they might be small but big in flavor, nutrition, and satisfaction. So, whether you're reaching for a snack to tide you over till dinner or adding a side to complement your meal, these plant-based options have got you covered. So, savor the goodness of plant-based eating, one snack or side at a time. And remember, the joy of plant-based eating is as much in the snacking and side dishes as in the main meals. So, let's continue to explore and enjoy the diverse world of plant-based foods.

### 8.2 Roasted Brussels Sprouts with Balsamic Glaze

*(Serves four people, 80-100 cal/serving, 4-6 brussel sprouts. Brussels sprouts are a nutritious vegetable rich in vitamins (especially vitamin C and vitamin K), fiber, and antioxidants. They are known for their potential health benefits, including supporting bone health and providing immune support).*

Brussels Sprout Preparation

Brussels sprouts, those tiny cabbages, are a treasure trove of nutrients. To prepare them for roasting, trim off the stem end and remove any yellow or damaged outer leaves. Cut each sprout in half from top to bottom. This speeds up the cooking process and creates a flat surface that gets nice and caramelized during roasting.

Once your sprouts are trimmed and halved, it's time to season them. Toss them in a bowl with a drizzle of olive oil and a sprinkle of salt and pepper. The oil helps them roast evenly, while the salt and pepper enhance their natural flavors.

Roasting Instructions

Spread the prepared Brussels sprouts on a baking sheet in

a single layer and cut side down. This ensures they roast evenly and get beautifully caramelized where they touch the pan.

Roast the sprouts in a preheated 400°F (200°C) oven for about 20-25 minutes until they're tender and the cut sides are golden brown. You can flip them halfway through for even browning, but this isn't strictly necessary.

<u>Balsamic Glaze Recipe</u>

While your Brussels sprouts are roasting perfectly, you can prepare the balsamic glaze. This sweet and tangy glaze is the perfect complement to the earthy sprouts, adding an extra layer of flavor that takes this dish to the next level.

Start by pouring 1 cup of balsamic vinegar into a small saucepan. Please bring it to a boil over medium heat, then reduce the heat to low and let it simmer. The vinegar will slowly reduce and thicken into a syrupy glaze. This process should take about 15-20 minutes. Keep an eye on it towards the end to prevent it from over-reducing and becoming too sticky.

Once your Brussels sprouts are roasted and your balsamic glaze is ready, drizzle the glaze over the sprouts. Toss them gently to ensure they're evenly coated. Your Roasted Brussels Sprouts with Balsamic Glaze are ready to be devoured. They make a delicious and nutritious side dish that's sure to impress with its complex flavors and elegant presentation. Enjoy them as part of a regular weeknight meal or serve them on a special occasion. Either way, this dish is a testament to the versatility and deliciousness of plant-based ingredients.

. . .

## 8.3 Sweet Potato Fries with Avocado Dip

*(Serves 4-6 people, 200-300 cal/serving. Sweet potatoes are a nutritious component of this recipe. They are rich in vitamins, particularly vitamin A (from beta-carotene), essential for eye health and immune function).*

## Sweet Potato Fries Recipe

Sweet potato fries bring a touch of sweetness to your snack time or as a side dish. These vibrant strips of deliciousness are simple to prepare. Start by selecting two medium-sized sweet potatoes. Sweet potatoes are a great source of fiber, vitamins, and minerals, making them a nutritious choice for your fries.

To remove dirt, begin by washing and scrubbing your sweet potatoes under cool running water. There's no need to peel the sweet potatoes—the skin is packed with nutrients and gives the fries a nice texture. Cut the sweet potatoes into even strips, about a quarter of an inch wide. This ensures that all your fries will cook evenly.

Once your fries are cut, toss them in a bowl with a tablespoon of olive oil. The oil helps them cook evenly and get a nice, crispy exterior. Season with a half teaspoon of paprika and a quarter teaspoon of garlic powder. These spices add a smoky, savory flavor that complements the sweetness of the potatoes.

### Baking Instructions

Spread the seasoned sweet potato strips out on a baking sheet. Please ensure they're in a single layer and not touching each other. This allows the hot oven air to circulate each fry, ensuring they get crispy on all sides.

Bake the fries in a preheated 425°F (220°C) oven for about 20-25 minutes. Halfway through the cooking time, take the baking sheet out and flip each fry. This helps them brown and crisp up evenly on all sides. Once your fries are golden brown and crispy, remove them from the oven and let them cool slightly.

<ins>Avocado Dip Recipe</ins>

You can prepare your avocado dip while your sweet potato fries are baking. This creamy, rich dip pairs perfectly with the sweet and savory fries, adding an extra layer of flavor and a nice contrast in texture.

Start with two ripe avocados. The avocados should give slightly when gently squeezed, indicating they're at the perfect ripeness. Cut the avocados in half, remove the pits, and scoop the flesh into a bowl. Avocados are a fantastic source of healthy fats, fiber, and essential nutrients.

Mash the avocado flesh with a fork until it's smooth but still has some chunks. Add the juice of one lime, a finely chopped small clove of garlic, and a quarter teaspoon of salt. The lime juice adds a bright, tangy flavor and helps keep the avocado from browning. The garlic brings a slight sharpness that complements the creaminess of the avocado—season with salt to bring all the flavors together.

Stir everything together until well combined. If you prefer a smoother dip, blend the ingredients in a food processor or blender until you reach your desired consistency. Your avocado dip is ready to be enjoyed with your sweet potato fries.

With your crispy sweet potato fries and creamy avocado dip ready, it's time to dig in. Each bite of the sweet, smoky fries dipped in the rich, tangy avocado dip is an explosion of flavors and textures in your mouth. It's a snack or side dish that's delicious and packed with nutrients. So savor this dish, knowing you're nourishing your body with every delightful bite. Enjoy the simplicity of plant-based eating and the joy it brings to your everyday meals.

### 8.4 BAKED FALAFEL BALLS

*(Serves 4-6 people, makes 16-20 falafel balls, 50-60 cal/ball. Chickpeas are the critical ingredient in falafel and are a good source of plant-based protein and dietary fiber. They also provide essential nutrients like folate, iron, and manganese).*

<u>Falafel Ingredients</u>

Falafel, a staple in Middle Eastern cuisine, are traditionally deep-fried balls or patties made from ground chickpeas or fava beans. Here, we're giving them a healthful twist by baking them instead of frying them. The result is a crunchy exterior, a tender interior, and all the flavorful goodness of traditional falafel, but with fewer calories and less fat.

To create your own baked falafel balls, gather these ingredients:

- 1 can (15 ounces) of chickpeas, drained and rinsed
- 1 large onion, finely chopped
- 2 cloves of garlic, minced
- 2 tablespoons of fresh parsley, finely chopped
- 2 tablespoons of fresh cilantro, finely chopped
- 1 teaspoon of ground cumin
- 1/4 teaspoon of ground coriander
- 1/2 teaspoon of salt
- 2 tablespoons of whole wheat flour
- 2 tablespoons of olive oil

Baking Instructions

First, preheat your oven to 375°F (190°C) and prepare a baking tray by lining it with parchment paper.

While the oven is heating, place the chickpeas, chopped onion, minced garlic, chopped parsley, chopped cilantro, ground cumin, ground coriander, salt, and whole wheat flour in a food processor. Blend the ingredients until they form a thick paste. If the mixture is too dry, add a little water, a tablespoon at a time.

Using your hands, shape the mixture into small balls, each about the size of a tablespoon. Arrange the falafel balls on your prepared baking tray and lightly brush them with olive oil. This will help them get a nice, golden color during baking.

Bake the falafel balls in the oven for about 20-25 minutes or until golden brown and crispy outside. Halfway through baking, carefully flip each falafel ball to ensure they brown evenly.

<u>Serving Suggestions</u>

Baked falafel balls are incredibly versatile and can be served in various ways. For a satisfying lunch, you could stuff them in a pita pocket with some fresh salad veggies and a drizzle of tahini sauce. They make great appetizers, served with a side of hummus or tzatziki for dipping. Or toss them into a salad for a protein-rich topping.

Each bite of these baked falafel balls is a delightful explosion of flavors and textures - the crunch of the exterior, the softness of the interior, the freshness of the herbs, and the warmth of the spices. They're a testament to the power of plant-based ingredients, proving that healthful eating doesn't have to compromise on flavor or satisfaction.

In this chapter, we've explored the diverse world of plant-based snacks and sides, from the creamy richness of hummus to the vibrant crunch of roasted Brussels sprouts, the sweet and savory delight of sweet potato fries to the hearty goodness of baked falafel balls. Each recipe showcases the versatility of plant-based ingredients and the limitless possibilities they offer. So, whether you're looking for a quick snack, a complement to your main meal, or a light lunch, these plant-based options have got you covered. So, savor the flavors, enjoy the process, and delight in their nourishment. Now, let's switch gears and explore the delightful world of global flavors.

# CHAPTER 9

## A CULINARY WORLD TOUR: GLOBAL FLAVORS, PLANT-BASED STYLE

Picture yourself as a global explorer, traversing continents, navigating diverse cultures, and savoring the unique flavors of each region. Now imagine doing all that without leaving your kitchen. Welcome to the world of global plant-based cuisine! In this chapter, we will take your taste buds on a journey around the globe, crafting plant-based versions of beloved international dishes—our first stop: the vibrant flavors of Thailand with a delightful Thai Green Curry with Tofu.

### 9.1 Thai Green Curry with Tofu

*(Serves four people, 300-400 cal/serving, one bowl. Tofu is a common ingredient in vegan and vegetarian diets and is a good source of plant-based protein).*

## Tofu Preparation

Tofu is a hearty, protein-rich centerpiece for our Thai Green Curry. Tofu, made from condensed soy milk, is a chameleon absorbing the flavors of the ingredients it's cooked with. To prepare tofu for our curry, start with one block of firm or extra-firm tofu. Drain the tofu and press it to remove excess water. This can be done using a tofu press or by wrapping the tofu in a clean kitchen towel and placing a heavy object on top for about 15 minutes. Once pressed, cut the tofu into bite-sized cubes.

## Green Curry Paste

The heart and soul of our Thai Green Curry is the curry paste. It's a fragrant blend of hot green chili, tangy lemongrass, aromatic galangal, and other herbs and spices. While store-bought green curry paste can be used conveniently, making your own lets you control the heat and flavor profile. To make your own, you'll need:

- 2 small green chilies, roughly chopped (reduce for less heat)
- 1 stalk lemongrass, thinly sliced
- 1-inch piece of galangal or ginger, peeled and chopped
- 2 shallots, peeled and chopped
- 2 cloves garlic, peeled
- A small bunch of fresh cilantro
- 1 teaspoon ground cumin
- 1 teaspoon ground coriander

Blend all ingredients in a food processor or mortar and pestle into a thick paste, adding water if needed.

Vegetable Selection

The beauty of a Thai Green Curry lies in its versatility. You can use a variety of vegetables based on your preference and what's available. Traditional choices include bell peppers, bamboo shoots, eggplants, and peas. However, feel free to get creative! Just cut your chosen veggies into bite-sized pieces for easy eating.

Coconut Milk Base

The base of our Thai Green Curry is coconut milk, which gives the dish its characteristic creamy texture and slight sweetness. Coconut milk also helps to balance the heat from the green curry paste. For the most decadent flavor, you'll need one can of full-fat coconut milk for this recipe.

Serving Suggestions

To assemble your Thai Green Curry, sauté your green

curry paste in a bit of oil for a few minutes to release its flavors. Add chopped vegetables and tofu, stirring to coat them in the paste. Pour in the coconut milk, bring to a boil, then reduce the heat and simmer until the vegetables are tender.

Thai Green Curry is traditionally served with steamed jasmine rice, a fragrant variety that complements the flavors of the curry. Scoop some rice into a bowl, spoon the curry over the top, and garnish with fresh Thai basil or cilantro.

As you take a bite of your Thai Green Curry with Tofu, let your senses revel in the symphony of flavors - the heat from the chili, the tang of the lemongrass, and the creaminess of the coconut milk. Each spoonful is a taste of Thailand, a celebration of its vibrant cuisine, and a testament to the power of plant-based ingredients. The best part? This is just the beginning of our culinary world tour. Stay tuned as we continue to explore the global flavors of plant-based cuisine. Bon appétit, or as they say in Thailand, ทานให้อร่อยนะ!

## 9.2 Mexican Black Bean Tacos

*(Serves four people, 100-150 cal/serving, one taco. Black beans are a good source of plant-based protein, fiber, and essential nutrients like iron and folate. They can contribute to a heart-healthy diet).*

## Black Bean Preparation

Our Mexican Black Bean Tacos start with the heart of the taco - the black beans. These small but mighty legumes are a powerhouse of protein and fiber, making them an excellent choice for plant-based meals. To prepare the black beans for your tacos, you'll need:

- 1 can (15 ounces) of black beans, drained and rinsed
- 1 small onion, finely chopped
- 2 cloves of garlic, minced
- 1 teaspoon ground cumin
- 1/2 teaspoon chili powder
- Salt to taste
- 1 tablespoon olive oil

Heat the olive oil in a skillet over medium heat. Add the chopped onion, cooking until it becomes translucent. Stir in the minced garlic, ground cumin, and chili powder, cooking for another minute until the spices are fragrant. Add the drained black beans and a pinch of salt, stirring to combine. Cook for a few more minutes until the beans are heated through.

<u>Taco Shell Choices</u>

When it comes to choosing your taco shell, you have several options. You could go with soft corn tortillas for a traditional Mexican feel. These are typically warmed on a dry skillet before serving. Hard-shell tacos are another great option if you prefer a bit of crunch. You can find both of these in most grocery stores. Consider using whole grain tortillas or lettuce leaves as your shell for a more nutritious option.

<u>Fresh Salsa Recipe</u>

A taco is not complete without salsa, a tangy and flavorful condiment that adds freshness. To make your fresh salsa, you'll need:

- 2 ripe tomatoes, finely diced
- 1 small onion, finely diced
- 1 jalapeno, seeds removed and finely diced
- Juice of 1 lime
- A handful of fresh cilantro, chopped.
- Salt to taste

Combine the diced tomatoes, onion, and jalapeno in a bowl. Add the lime juice and chopped cilantro, stirring to combine—season with salt to taste. The salsa should be tangy, with a bit of heat from the jalapeno, and the cilantro should add a refreshing note.

### Guacamole Recipe

Another essential component of a great taco is guacamole, a creamy and delicious spread made from ripe avocados. For your guacamole, you'll need:

- 2 ripe avocados
- Juice of 1 lime
- 1 small onion, finely diced
- 1 clove of garlic, minced
- Salt to taste

Halve the avocados, remove the pits, and scoop the flesh into a bowl. Add the lime juice and use a fork to mash the avocado until it's as smooth or chunky as you like. Stir in the diced onion and minced garlic, and season with salt to taste. Guacamole adds a creamy element to the tacos, balancing the heat of the salsa and the hearty black beans.

### Serving and Presentation Tips

With all your components ready, it's time to assemble your Black Bean Tacos. Start by spreading a spoonful of guacamole onto your chosen taco shell. Top with the black bean mixture and a spoonful of fresh salsa.

Arrange your tacos on a platter and garnish with fresh cilantro leaves or lime wedges for a beautiful presentation. The vibrant colors of the ingredients make the tacos visually appealing, and the variety of textures and flavors will surely delight your palate.

These Black Bean Tacos are a great way to bring the flavors of Mexico to your kitchen. They're not only delicious and satisfying but also packed with nutritious ingredients. These tacos will surely be a hit, whether for a casual weeknight dinner or a festive gathering with friends. Enjoy the process of making them, and even more, enjoy eating them!

## 9.3 Italian Vegetable Lasagna

*(Serves 6-8 people, 300-400 cal/serving. Bell peppers, zucchini, eggplant, and spinach are rich in vitamins, minerals, and dietary fiber, offering various health benefits).*

Vegetable Selection and Preparation

We'll use a medley of vibrant vegetables in our rendition of an Italian classic, the vegetable lasagna. Choose colorful and nutrition-packed veggies such as bell peppers, zucchini, eggplant, and spinach. Slice the bell peppers and zucchini into thin strips and chop the eggplant into small cubes. For the spinach, a quick rinse and drain will do. Saute your bell peppers, zucchini, and eggplant in olive oil over medium heat until tender and slightly caramelized. The spinach can be wilted in the pan with a dash of water.

Tomato Sauce Recipe

To create the rich tomato sauce that will be layered in our lasagna, you will need:

- 1 can (28 ounces) of crushed tomatoes
- 1 small onion, finely chopped
- 2 cloves of garlic, minced
- A handful of fresh basil leaves, torn.
- Salt and pepper to taste
- 1 tablespoon of olive oil

Start by gently cooking the chopped onion and minced garlic in the olive oil until soft and fragrant. Stir in the crushed tomatoes and torn basil leaves, and season with salt and pepper. Let the sauce simmer on low heat for about 20 minutes to allow the flavors to meld together.

Vegan Bechamel Sauce Recipe

In traditional lasagna, a creamy bechamel sauce is layered with the tomato sauce. We'll use plant-based milk and nutritional yeast to create a plant-based version for a cheesy flavor. You'll need:

- 2 cups of unsweetened almond milk
- 2 tablespoons of olive oil
- 2 tablespoons of all-purpose flour
- 2 tablespoons of nutritional yeast
- Salt and nutmeg to taste

Heat the olive oil in a saucepan and stir in the flour to create a roux. Gradually whisk in the almond milk until smooth. Add the nutritional yeast, a pinch of nutmeg, and salt. Continue to cook the sauce, stirring often, until it thickens to the consistency of a traditional bechamel sauce.

Layering Techniques

Now comes the fun part - layering your lasagna. Start with a thin layer of tomato sauce at the bottom of your baking dish to prevent sticking. Next, arrange a layer of lasagna noodles, ensuring they overlap slightly. Spread your bechamel sauce over the noodles, followed by a layer of sauteed vegetables. Repeat these layers until all ingredients are used up, finishing with a layer of tomato and bechamel sauce on top for a beautiful golden finish.

Baking Instructions

Cover your lasagna with foil and bake in a preheated oven at 375°F (190°C) for about 25 minutes. This allows the flavors to meld together and the noodles to cook. After 25 minutes, remove the foil and bake for another 10-15 minutes or until the top is golden and bubbling. Allow your lasagna to rest a few minutes before serving to make cutting and serving easier.

There you have it – a hearty, flavorful, and nutrition-packed Italian Vegetable Lasagna. Each bite delivers a burst of savory tomato sauce, creamy bechamel, tender vegetables, and satisfying pasta. It's a dish that proves just how delicious and comforting plant-based eating can be.

### 9.4 Indian Vegetable Biryani

*(Serves 4-6 people, 300-400 cal/serving, medium plate. Basmati rice, commonly used in biryani, is a fragrant and long-grain rice variety. It provides carbohydrates for energy and is a good source of vitamins and minerals like B vitamins and selenium).*

Basmati Rice Preparation

Let's create the Indian Vegetable Biryani by preparing the

basmati rice. This aromatic grain is the backbone of biryani, offering a light, fluffy texture that beautifully complements the rich flavors of the dish. Rinse 2 cups of basmati rice under cold water until the water runs clear. This step removes excess starch and helps achieve a non-sticky texture once cooked. Transfer the rinsed rice to a pot, add 4 cups of water, and bring to a boil. Reduce the heat, cover the pot, and let the rice simmer for 15-20 minutes, or until the grains are tender and all the water is absorbed.

Spice Blend Creation

The soul of biryani resides in its unique spice blend, forming a melody of flavors that dance on your palate. In a small bowl, combine one teaspoon of ground cumin, turmeric, coriander, and garam masala. Add a half teaspoon of chili powder for a hint of heat and a pinch of saffron for a touch of luxury. Stir the spices together until they're well blended.

Vegetable Selection

Every forkful of biryani promises a treasure trove of colorful and nutritious vegetables. Traditional biryani often includes a mix of peas, carrots, potatoes, and cauliflower. However, you can add your favorite vegetables or what you have. Just make sure to cut them into bite-sized pieces for uniform cooking.

Layering and Cooking Process

Now, it's time to bring all the elements of the biryani together. Heat 2 tablespoons of olive oil over medium heat in a large pot. Add one finely chopped onion and two minced cloves of garlic, cooking until the onion is translucent. Stir in your spice blend, cooking for a minute to release the aroma of the spices. Add your chosen vegetables, stirring well to coat them in the spices.

Pour in a cup of vegetable broth and bring the mixture to a simmer. Let it cook for 10-15 minutes or until the vegetables are tender. Layer your cooked basmati rice over the vegetable mixture, spreading it out evenly. Cover the pot, reduce the heat to low, and let it cook for about 20 minutes. This allows the flavors of the spices to infuse the rice and the vegetables to meld together.

Garnishing and Serving Suggestions

Your Indian Vegetable Biryani is nearly ready to be savored. Before serving, garnish your biryani with a handful of fresh, chopped coriander for a burst of freshness and a sprinkle of toasted almond flakes for a satisfying crunch.

To serve, scoop a generous portion of biryani into a bowl or onto a plate. The vegetables' vibrant colors and the spices' aromatic allure make this dish as appealing to the eye as it is to the palate. Each bite celebrates flavors and textures, showcasing the richness and diversity of Indian cuisine.

As we wrap up this culinary world tour, remember that each recipe is an invitation to explore and celebrate the diversity and richness of global cuisines, all through a plant-based lens. Whether you're savoring the creamy comfort of Thai Green Curry, the hearty satisfaction of Mexican Black Bean Tacos, the rich flavors of Italian Vegetable Lasagna, or the vibrant allure of Indian Vegetable Biryani, you're experiencing the joy and satisfaction of plant-based eating. With each dish, you're nourishing your body, expanding your culinary horizons, and taking part in a global tradition of food and flavor. So, here's to the joy of cooking, the pleasure of eating, and the adventure of exploring global flavors, one plant-based dish at a time. Now, let's continue to the next delicious chapter.

# CHAPTER 10

## SWEET ENDINGS: PLANT-BASED DESSERTS AND BAKED GOODS

Imagine this: you've just enjoyed a delicious, nutrition-packed plant-based meal. You sit back, satisfied, feeling nourished and energized. But something's missing. Something sweet, something decadent, something to signal the end of the meal and leave a lingering taste of indulgence on your palate. You need dessert. But not just any dessert. A plant-based dessert that's as healthful as it is delicious. A dessert that brings a sweet ending to your meal while continuing to nourish your body with whole, plant-based ingredients. Welcome to the delightful world of plant-based desserts and baked goods.

Let's start with a dessert that's as surprising as it is scrumptious - a Chocolate Avocado Mousse. Yes, you read that right. Avocado, the creamy, nutrient-packed fruit, is about to be transformed into a rich, velvety mousse that will satisfy your sweet tooth.

### 10.1 CHOCOLATE AVOCADO MOUSSE

*(Serves 2-4 people, 150-200 cal/serving, small bowl. Avocado is the crucial ingredient in this dessert, providing healthy monounsaturated fats, fiber, and various vitamins and minerals, including potassium, vitamin K, and folate).*

Avocado Selection and Preparation

Choosing the right avocado is critical to achieving the perfect texture for your mousse. You want an avocado that's ripe but not overripe. It should yield slightly to gentle pressure but not feel mushy. Once you've selected the perfect avocado, cut it in half, remove the pit, and scoop out the flesh. The avocado's creamy texture gives the mousse its incredibly smooth, velvety texture.

### Sweetening Options

You'll need a sweetener to add sweetness to the mousse. Maple syrup is an excellent choice for its robust sweetness and subtle flavor notes that complement the chocolate. You could also use agave syrup for a lighter, more neutral sweetness. Start with a tablespoon and adjust according to your taste.

### Chocolate Selection

Chocolate is the show's star in this mousse, so choose a high-quality one. A bar of dark chocolate with 70-80% cocoa content is an excellent choice for its rich, intense flavor and health benefits. It's packed with antioxidants and gives the mousse its deep chocolatey taste. Melt about 100g of the chocolate in a double boiler or microwave, ensuring it's smooth and free of lumps.

### Blending Instructions

Now, it's time to bring it all together. Combine the avocado flesh, your chosen sweetener, and the melted chocolate in a blender or food processor. Blend until everything is well combined and the mixture is smooth and creamy. You might need to scrape down the sides a few times to ensure everything gets blended.

### Serving Suggestions

Your Chocolate Avocado Mousse is ready to be savored. Spoon it into individual serving dishes and pop them into the fridge to chill for about an hour. This allows the mousse to firm up slightly and the flavors to meld together.

When you're ready to serve, consider adding a few toppings for an extra touch of indulgence. A dollop of coconut whipped cream, a sprinkle of chopped nuts, or some fresh berries would all make lovely additions. Each spoonful of this mousse celebrates creamy, chocolatey goodness, a testament to the versatility of plant-based ingredients, and a delightful way to end a meal. So, indulge in this sweet treat, knowing you're nourishing your body with every delicious bite. Enjoy the contrast between the rich mousse and the crunchy toppings, the subtle sweetness perfectly balanced by the bitterness of the dark chocolate. It's a dessert experience that's as satisfying as it is nourishing.

Indeed, plant-based desserts and baked goods are more than just a sweet ending to a meal. They're an opportunity to continue nourishing your body with whole foods, to satisfy your sweet tooth healthfully, and to explore the limitless possibilities of plant-based ingredients. So, whether you're whipping up a decadent Chocolate Avocado Mousse for a dinner party or simply treating yourself to a sweet indulgence after a long day, these plant-based desserts and baked goods will surely delight. Enjoy the creativity, savor the flavors, and celebrate the joy of plant-based eating, one sweet spoonful at a time.

### 10.2 Vegan Banana Bread

*(Serves 8-12 people, 150-250 cal/serving, one slice. Bananas are the star ingredient, providing natural sweetness, fiber, potassium, and essential vitamins and minerals).*

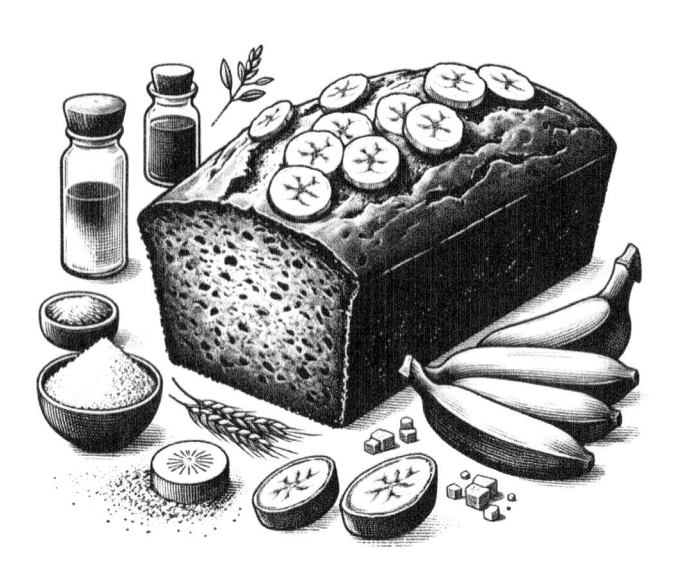

Banana Ripeness

The key to moist, sweet vegan banana bread begins with the bananas. The perfect bananas for this recipe are those that many might consider overripe. Look for bananas with peels that are heavily speckled with brown or even entirely brown. At this stage of ripeness, bananas are at their sweetest, with flavor notes that are almost reminiscent of honey. Their texture is also ideal, melting into a sticky, sweet pulp that will add moisture to your banana bread.

Flour Options

Next, consider your flour options. While all-purpose flour is a common choice, whole wheat flour can provide additional fiber and a slightly nutty flavor to your banana bread. For a gluten-free option, consider oat flour or a gluten-free flour blend. If you're feeling adventurous, you can experiment with almond or spelt flour. Remember that different flours may alter the texture of your banana bread, so don't be afraid to experiment to find your perfect blend!

Sweetening Choices

When it comes to sweetening your banana bread, you have several options. If your bananas are exceptionally ripe, they may provide enough sweetness. If you prefer a bit sweeter banana bread, consider adding a natural sweetener like maple syrup or agave nectar. These liquid sweeteners can also add moisture to your banana bread. Organic cane sugar or coconut sugar are also excellent choices for a more traditional approach.

- 3 ripe bananas (about 1 1/2 cups mashed)
- 1/3 cup melted coconut oil or vegetable oil
- 1/2 cup maple syrup or agave nectar (you can adjust based on your sweetness preference)
- 1/4 cup plant-based milk (such as almond milk, soy milk, or oat milk)
- 1 teaspoon vanilla extract
- 2 cups all-purpose flour (for a gluten-free version, you can use a gluten-free flour blend)
- 1/2 teaspoon salt
- 1 teaspoon baking soda
- 1/2 teaspoon ground cinnamon (optional for added flavor)
- 1/2 cup walnuts or pecans (optional, for added texture and flavor)

Baking Instructions

Now, let's get baking! Preheat your oven to 350°F (175°C)

and prepare a loaf pan by lightly greasing it and lining it with parchment paper. In a large bowl, mash your ripe bananas until you have a relatively smooth pulp. Add your chosen sweetener, a flax egg (1 tablespoon of ground flaxseed mixed with 2.5 tablespoons of water), and a bit of vanilla extract for depth of flavor. Whisk together your chosen flour, baking soda, and a pinch of salt in a separate bowl. Gradually add your dry ingredients to the banana mixture, stirring until combined.

Pour your banana bread batter into your prepared loaf pan, smoothing the top with a spatula. Bake in your preheated oven for about 60 minutes or until a toothpick inserted into the center of the loaf comes out clean. If your banana bread begins to brown too quickly, you can lightly cover it with aluminum foil for the remainder of the baking time.

Storage Tips

Once your banana bread is baked, cool it in the loaf pan for about 10 minutes, then use the edges of the parchment paper to lift the loaf from the pan and place it on a wire rack to cool completely. Vegan banana bread can be stored at room temperature for up to 3 days or in the refrigerator for up to a week. For more extended storage, consider slicing the loaf and freezing individual slices. Whether enjoyed fresh from the oven or defrosted from the freezer, your vegan banana bread will surely be a delicious treat. Enjoy a slice as a sweet end to a meal or as a satisfying snack any time of day.

**10.3 COCONUT CHIA PUDDING**

*(Serves 2-4 people, 150-200 cal/serving, small bowl. Chia seeds*

*are a vital ingredient in Coconut Chia Pudding. They are a good source of fiber, omega-3 fatty acids, and various vitamins and minerals).*

Chia Seed Basics

Diving into plant-based desserts, let's spotlight a humble yet powerful ingredient - chia seeds. Originating from the desert plant Salvia hispanica, these tiny seeds pack a punch of nutrients. They are rich in omega-3 fatty acids, fiber, and protein, making them a stellar addition to a plant-based diet. But their magic doesn't stop there. When soaked in liquid, chia seeds expand and form a gel-like coating around them, which gives our pudding its unique texture.

Coconut Milk Selection

Next on our ingredient list is coconut milk. This creamy, tropical liquid will form the base of our chia pudding, lending it a rich texture and subtle sweetness. While several varieties of coconut milk are available in the market, opt for full-fat canned coconut milk for this recipe. Its higher fat content gives our pudding a lusciously creamy consistency.

Sweetening and Flavoring Choices

Now, let's add a touch of sweetness to our pudding. While coconut milk has a subtle sweetness, a hint of extra sweetener can make our pudding taste like an authentic dessert. A natural sweetener like maple syrup or agave nectar works well, providing sweetness without overpowering the delicate flavors of coconut and chia. For flavoring, a splash of pure vanilla extract can enhance the overall taste of the pudding, its floral notes pairing beautifully with the tropical flavor of coconut.

Preparation and Resting Time

The preparation of coconut chia pudding is a breeze. Combine 1/4 cup of chia seeds, 1 cup of coconut milk, your chosen sweetener, and vanilla extract in a bowl. Stir well to ensure there are no clumps of chia seeds. Cover the bowl and place it in the refrigerator. The chia seeds will absorb the coconut milk, expanding and forming a gel-like coating. For the pudding to reach the right consistency, it must rest for at least 4 hours, ideally overnight. This allows the chia seeds ample time to soak up the liquid and achieve a pudding-like consistency.

Serving and Topping Ideas

With the coconut chia pudding chilled and ready, it's time for the final flourish - the toppings. Toppings not only liven up the appearance of the pudding but also add a contrast of textures. Fresh fruits like berries or sliced bananas add natural sweetness and a pop of color. A sprinkle of toasted coconut flakes contributes a delightful crunch and reinforces the coconut flavor. Nut lovers can add a handful of toasted almonds or walnuts for added crunch and healthy fats.

The beauty of this coconut chia pudding lies in its simplicity. A handful of wholesome ingredients come together to create a dessert that's as nourishing as it is delicious. Each spoonful invites a dance of textures - the creaminess of the pudding, the crunch of the toppings, and the pop of the fresh fruit. It's a sweet ending that's sure to satisfy without veering away from the goodness of plant-based ingredients. Enjoy the subtle sweetness, the tropical hint of coconut, and the satisfaction of creating a dessert that's as good for your body as it is for your taste buds. And remember, the world of plant-based desserts is as vast and varied as the plant kingdom itself - there's always a new flavor to taste, a new texture to experience, and a new recipe to create. So, here's to the sweet, indulgent, and nourishing world of plant-based desserts. Enjoy every bite!

## 10.4 Apple Crisp with Oat Topping

*(Serves 6-8 people, 150-250 cal/serving, medium bowl. The oat topping often contains rolled oats, which are a good source of fiber and provide complex carbohydrates for sustained energy).*

### Apple Selection and Preparation

Selecting the suitable apples can make all the difference in your apple crisp. You want apples that will hold their shape during baking but break down enough to become tender. Granny Smith apples are famous for their tart flavor and firm texture. Honeycrisp or Golden Delicious apples also work well. Once you've chosen your apples, you must peel, core, and slice them. Aiming for thin even slices to ensure the apples cook evenly is a good rule of thumb.

### Oat Topping Recipe

The oat topping is what sets an apple crisp apart. It adds a delightful crunch and a layer of flavor that perfectly complements the tender apples. To make it, combine 1 cup of old-fashioned oats, 1/2 cup of brown sugar, 1/2 cup of all-purpose flour, and 1/2 teaspoon of cinnamon. Cut in 1/2 cup of cold vegan butter, working it in until the mixture resembles coarse crumbs. The butter should be evenly distributed throughout the oat mixture, creating little clumps that will crisp up beautifully in the oven.

Baking Instructions

To assemble your apple crisp, arrange your sliced apples in a baking dish. Sprinkle a tablespoon of lemon juice over the apples to prevent browning and add a bit of tanginess. Next, evenly distribute the oat topping over the apples, covering them in a thick blanket of crumbly goodness.

Bake your apple crisp in a preheated 350°F (175°C) oven for about 45 minutes, until the apples are bubbling and the topping is golden brown. If the topping starts to brown too quickly, you can cover the dish with a piece of aluminum foil for the remainder of the baking time.

Serving Suggestions

There's nothing quite like a warm apple crisp right out of the oven. The aroma of baked apples and cinnamon wafting through your kitchen is a sensory delight. Scoop a generous portion of the apple crisp into a bowl for serving. Consider adding a scoop of vegan vanilla ice cream on top. As it melts, it creates a creamy sauce that mingles with the juicy apples and crunchy topping. A drizzle of caramel sauce can add an extra layer of indulgence.

Storage Tips

If you're lucky enough to have leftovers, apple crisp can be stored in the refrigerator for up to four days. Cover the baking dish with plastic wrap or transfer the leftover apple crisp to an airtight container. When you're ready to enjoy it again, you can eat it cold, let it come to room temperature, or warm it up in the oven. If reheating in the oven, cover with foil and heat at 350°F (175°C) until warm.

There you have it - a comforting, delicious, and entirely plant-based apple crisp that will satisfy your sweet tooth. Each spoonful brings together tender apples, a sweet and crunchy oat topping, and the warmth of cinnamon - a trio of flavors that's as comforting as it is delicious. It's a dessert that celebrates the simplicity of plant-based ingredients and the joy of creating something genuinely delightful from them. Enjoy the process, savor the flavors, and indulge in the sweet satisfaction of a well-made dessert.

As we end this chapter, remember that plant-based desserts and baked goods are not just sweet treats. They continue the nourishment and enjoyment we get from eating plant-based foods. Each recipe, each ingredient, and each sweet bite is a celebration of the bounty and variety of whole plant foods. So, whether you're baking a loaf of banana bread, whipping up a chocolate avocado mousse, assembling a coconut chia pudding, or baking an apple crisp, know that you're creating something that's not only delicious but also nourishing. Now, let's move on to the next exciting chapter in our plant-based culinary adventure.

# CHAPTER 11

## BLEND IT UP: PLANT-BASED BEVERAGES AND SMOOTHIES

Each day is a new canvas, a fresh opportunity to infuse our bodies with nourishment and vitality. What if we begin by pouring ourselves a glass of wellness, a concoction that's as reviving as the morning sun? A vibrant, plant-based beverage or smoothie can be a delicious way to kickstart our day, offering an abundance of nutrients in every sip. From the fresh greens in your detox smoothie to the warming spices in your pumpkin latte, these beverages celebrate nature's bounty and the vitality it brings.

Let's start our exploration of plant-based beverages with a smoothie that's as revitalizing as a spring morning - a Green Detox Smoothie. This smoothie is a blend of nutrient-dense greens, refreshing fruits, and hydrating liquids, all coming together to cleanse and rejuvenate your body. So, let's gather our ingredients and blend!

### 11.1 GREEN DETOX SMOOTHIE

*(Serves 1-2 people, 150-250 cal/serving. Green detox smoothies often include leafy greens like spinach, kale, or chard. These greens are packed with vitamins, minerals, and antioxidants).*

Green Vegetable Choices

Our Green Detox Smoothie starts with a generous handful of leafy green vegetables. These greens are a powerhouse of nutrients, offering a wealth of vitamins, minerals, and fiber. With its mild flavor and high iron content, Spinach makes an excellent choice. Kale, another nutrient-dense green, brings a slightly peppery note to our smoothie. Other options include romaine lettuce,

Swiss chard, or a mixture of your favorite greens. Remember to wash your greens thoroughly before using them.

### Fruit Pairings

The addition of fruit to our smoothie not only adds sweetness but also provides a range of antioxidants. Apples, with their crisp sweetness, pair well with the fresh greens. Citrus fruits like oranges or grapefruits can add a tangy twist and boost vitamin C. If you prefer a creamier smoothie, a ripe banana or some avocado can do the trick. The naturally sweet and creamy profile of these fruits balances the earthy flavor of the greens.

### Liquid Options

The choice of liquid in your smoothie can influence its overall flavor and nutritional profile. Almond milk or coconut water could lend a subtle nutty or tropical hint while enhancing the smoothie's texture. If you prefer a more neutral taste, filtered water works just as well.

### Optional Add-Ins

To boost the nutritional value of your smoothie, consider adding a spoonful of flax or chia seeds. These seeds are rich in Omega-3 fatty acids, fiber, and protein. A scoop of plant-based protein powder can give your smoothie an extra protein punch, making it a more filling option for breakfast or post-workout recovery.

### Blending and Serving Tips

Start by adding the liquid, the greens, the fruits, and any optional add-ins to your blender. This order allows the blender to process the ingredients efficiently, creating a smoother consistency. Blend until all the ingredients are well combined, and the smoothie is creamy.

For serving, pour your Green Detox Smoothie into a glass or a mason jar if you're on the go. You might want to garnish it with a slice of citrus or chia seeds for an extra touch. Enjoy this smoothie as a refreshing start to your day, a post-workout refuel, or a mid-afternoon pick-me-up.

So, there you have it, a Green Detox Smoothie - a glass of revitalizing goodness, a testament to the power of plant-based ingredients. Each sip delivers a symphony of flavors and a rush of nutrients, offering a delicious and refreshing way to nourish your body. As you enjoy this smoothie, consider its variety of ingredients, each contributing its unique nutritional profile and flavor to create a harmonious blend. It's a reminder of the diversity and richness of plant-based foods and the countless ways they can be combined to create delicious and nutritious beverages.

### 11.2 ALMOND MILK HOT CHOCOLATE

*(Serves 1-2 people, 100-150 cal/serving. Almond milk is a dairy-free alternative to traditional milk, making this hot chocolate suitable for those with lactose intolerance or following a vegan diet).*

### Almond Milk Selection

Choosing the suitable almond milk lays the foundation for our heart-warming hot chocolate. Opt for unsweetened almond milk in a market filled with many choices. This variant allows you to control the sweetness of your hot chocolate and reduces unnecessary sugar intake. Also, ensure it's free from additives, carrageenan, and artificial sweeteners. If you're feeling adventurous, homemade almond milk can take your hot chocolate up a notch with its fresh and subtly nutty flavor.

### Chocolate Selection

The core of our hot chocolate is, of course, the chocolate itself. Dark chocolate is an excellent choice with its deep, intense flavor. Look for a high-quality dark chocolate with 70% or higher cocoa content. This ensures your hot chocolate is rich in flavor and packed with antioxidants. Break the chocolate into small pieces to help it melt evenly in the warm almond milk.

### Sweetening Options

Sweetness binds the flavors of almond milk and dark chocolate together. While the dark chocolate does contribute some sweetness, a touch more can enhance the overall flavor. Opt for a natural sweetener like pure maple syrup or raw honey. These sweeteners not only add sweetness but also bring their unique flavors. Start with a small amount and adjust it to suit your palate.

### Heating Instructions

The key to a perfect hot chocolate lies in slow, gentle heating. This helps to preserve the delicate flavors of the almond milk and dark chocolate. Pour your almond milk into a saucepan and place it over medium heat. Once the almond milk is warm, add the dark chocolate pieces. Stir continuously until the chocolate melts into the almond milk, creating a smooth, uniform mixture. Be careful not to let the mixture boil, as this can affect the texture and flavor of your hot chocolate.

### Serving Suggestions

With your almond milk hot chocolate ready, let's turn our attention to serving. Pour the hot chocolate into a mug, taking a moment to appreciate the rich aroma wafting up. Consider a dollop of coconut whipped cream on top for a dairy-free, decadent touch. A sprinkle of cinnamon or nutmeg can add warmth and complexity. If you're serving this for a special occasion, garnish with a cinnamon stick or a dusting of cocoa powder for a visually appealing and aromatic addition.

There it is, a mug of almond milk hot chocolate, ready to warm your hands and delight your senses. From the creamy almond milk to the rich dark chocolate, each ingredient contributes to creating a comforting beverage that's as nourishing as it is delicious. So wrap your hands around the mug, take a slow sip, and savor the moment. Here's to cozy afternoons, quiet moments, and the simple pleasure of a well-made hot chocolate.

## 11.3 BERRY BLAST SMOOTHIE

*(Serves one person, 200-250 cal/serving. Berries are packed with antioxidants, which help combat oxidative stress in the body, potentially reducing the risk of chronic diseases and promoting overall health).*

### Berry Selection

This Berry Blast Smoothie's heroes are undoubtedly the berries themselves. Their vibrant colors hint at the wealth of nutrients they carry, including antioxidants that promote overall health. There's a world of berries, each bringing unique flavor and health benefits to the mix. Strawberries impart a classic, sweet-tart flavor and are loaded with vitamin C. Blueberries, with their deep blue hue, contribute a subtle, wine-like flavor and are packed with antioxidants. Raspberries add a delightful tang and a boost of fiber. Frozen berries work just as well as fresh ones for convenience and a chilled effect. Feel free to use a single type of berry or a mix of your favorites.

### Liquid Options

The choice of liquid can influence your smoothie's texture and flavor profile. Almond milk complements the berries beautifully and contributes to a creamy texture with its subtle, nutty flavor. Coconut water, on the other hand, lends a tropical note and a more refreshing, lighter texture. If you prefer a creamier and protein-packed smoothie, opt for soy milk. Each offers a unique twist, so choose according to your preference.

### Sweetening Choices

Berries, while flavorful, can sometimes be quite tart. A splash of sweetness can balance this tartness and enhance the overall flavor of the smoothie. Consider natural sweeteners like raw honey, which adds a floral sweetness, or pure maple syrup for its caramel notes. If your berries are already quite sweet, you might not need additional sweetener. Remember, you can always adjust the sweetness to your liking at the end.

Optional Add-Ins

Consider adding a tablespoon or two of your favorite superfoods for an extra nutritional boost. Chia seeds or flaxseeds can increase fiber content and provide beneficial Omega-3 fatty acids. A handful of spinach or kale blends well and adds valuable vitamins and minerals without altering the fruity flavor. A scoop of plant-based protein powder or Greek yogurt can make your smoothie filling, perfect for a quick breakfast or post-workout drink.

Blending and Serving Tips

To create your Berry Blast Smoothie, start by adding the liquid to your blender, the berries, any optional add-ins, and finally, your sweetener. This order allows the blender to process the ingredients quickly, creating a smoother consistency. Blend until all the ingredients are well combined, and the smoothie is creamy.

Serving your smoothie can be as simple or as creative as you like. Pour your Berry Blast Smoothie into a glass or a mason jar for a portable option. Garnish with a few whole berries or a sprig of fresh mint for a flair. This smoothie is best enjoyed immediately to benefit from the berries' freshness and prevent the smoothie from separating. Relish the harmony of flavors, the refreshing taste, and the healthful ingredients that make up this Berry Blast Smoothie. It's truly a delight to the senses and a testament to the magic of plant-based ingredients. Enjoy the burst of berry goodness, the smooth, satisfying texture, and the subtle sweetness that dances on your palate. Here's to the simple pleasure of a well-made smoothie, a glassful of nourishment, and a vibrant start to your day.

## 11.4 Spiced Pumpkin Latte

*(Serves 1-2 people, 150-250 cal/serving. The main ingredient is pumpkin puree, which is rich in vitamins and minerals, particularly vitamin A and potassium).*

<u>Pumpkin Puree Basics</u>

Warm, comforting, and delightfully seasonal, a Spiced Pumpkin Latte captures the essence of fall in a mug. The star ingredient, pumpkin puree, brings a touch of sweetness and a velvety texture to this beverage. If you've only ever used pumpkin puree in pies, you're in for a treat.

Making your pumpkin puree is simple and rewarding. Cut a small pumpkin into halves or quarters, remove the seeds and stringy bits, and roast in the oven until the flesh is tender. Scoop out the flesh and puree it in a blender or food processor until smooth. If you're short on time, canned pumpkin puree works just as well. Just make sure you're using pure pumpkin puree and not pumpkin pie filling with added sugars and spices.

### Spice Blend Creation

The "spice" in Spiced Pumpkin Latte comes from a warm and aromatic blend of spices. Ground cinnamon brings a sweet and woody flavor, ground ginger adds a bit of heat, and cloves lend a warm, sweet aroma. Nutmeg, with its sweet and nutty flavor, rounds out the blend. Stir together equal parts of these spices and adjust according to your taste. The result is a homemade pumpkin spice blend that is versatile and full of flavor.

### Milk Options

Your choice of milk can significantly influence the texture and flavor of your latte. Full-fat cow's milk is a classic choice for a rich, creamy latte. But in the spirit of plant-based beverages, you might opt for a non-dairy alternative. Almond milk, with its subtle nuttiness, or soy milk, known for its creamy texture and high protein content, are excellent choices. Coconut milk can lend a tropical twist and a velvety texture to your latte.

### Sweetening Choices

While the pumpkin puree and spices bring a natural sweetness to the latte, a touch of added sweetener can enhance these flavors. Natural sweeteners like pure maple syrup or agave nectar work beautifully, adding a hint of caramel-like sweetness. Remember to add sweetener gradually, tasting as you go. This allows you to control the sweetness level to your liking.

### Preparation and Serving Suggestions

Heat your milk in a saucepan over medium heat to create your Spiced Pumpkin Latte. Add a couple of tablespoons of pumpkin puree and your homemade spice blend to the warm milk, whisking to combine. Allow this mixture to heat until it's steaming, then remove from heat and stir in your chosen sweetener.

Add a shot of espresso or a half cup of strong-brewed coffee to your latte for a caffeine kick. But if you're not a coffee drinker, the pumpkin-spice milk is just as delicious on its own.

To serve, pour your Spiced Pumpkin Latte into a large mug. Top it off with a dollop of coconut whipped cream and a sprinkle of cinnamon for a café-style treat at home. Each sip is a comforting blend of sweet pumpkin, warming spices, and creamy milk—an indulgence you can feel good about.

There you have it, a selection of plant-based beverages that are nourishing and delicious. From detoxifying green smoothies to indulgent hot chocolate and refreshing berry blasts to comforting pumpkin lattes, these recipes showcase the versatility and delight of plant-based beverages. They're a testament that nourishing your body can be a delicious endeavor. So, pour yourself a glass of plant-based goodness, savor the flavors, and toast to your health. Let's continue our culinary adventure as we focus on an essential aspect of any diet - adapting traditional recipes to fit a plant-based lifestyle.

# CHAPTER 12

## MAKING OVER YOUR FAVORITES: PLANT-BASED STYLE

Imagine the comforting smell of a pizza baking in the oven, the sight of melted cheese stretching with each slice, the satisfying crunch of the crust, and the explosion of flavors with every bite. Now, imagine all of this, but plant-based. Yes, you heard it right! Your favorite comfort food can be enjoyed in a plant-based version that's just as comforting, satisfying, and delicious. It might even taste better. Let's start creating your very own Plant-Based Pizza with Cashew Cheese.

### 12.1 Plant-Based Pizza with Cashew Cheese

*(Serves 2-4 people, makes 2x12 inch pizzas, 500-600 cal/pie. Making your pizza dough from scratch allows you to control the ingredients, making it suitable for dietary preferences or restric-*

*tions. Homemade pizza dough typically tastes fresher and can have a better texture than store-bought options).*

### Pizza Dough Recipe

The foundation of any great pizza is the crust. A homemade pizza crust is easier to make than you think and worth the effort.

Ingredients:

- 1 tsp sugar
- 1 1/2 cups warm water (110 degrees F/45 degrees C)
- 2 1/4 tsp active dry yeast
- 3 1/2 cups bread flour
- 2 tbsp olive oil

- 2 tsp salt

Instructions:

1. Start by dissolving the sugar in warm water in a medium-sized bowl. Sprinkle yeast over the top and let it sit for about 10 minutes until it's foamy.
2. Stir the yeast mixture with a spoon and add the flour, salt, and olive oil. Mix until the dough starts to come together.
3. Place the dough on a well-floured surface and knead it for about 5 minutes until it is smooth and elastic.
4. Lightly oil a large bowl and place the dough in it, turning to coat with oil. Cover the bowl with a clean dishcloth and let the dough rise in a warm area until it doubles in size, about 2 hours.

Cashew Cheese Recipe

The next component is the cheese. Cashew cheese is a creamy, tangy, and incredibly delicious plant-based cheese alternative that melts beautifully on pizza.

Ingredients:

- 1 cup raw cashews
- 1/4 cup nutritional yeast
- Juice of 1 lemon
- 1/2 cup water
- Salt to taste

Instructions:

1. Soak the cashews in water for at least 4 hours or overnight if you have time. This softens the cashews and ensures a smoother texture for the cheese.
2. Drain and rinse the cashews, then place them in a blender. Add the nutritional yeast, lemon juice, water, and salt.
3. Blend until the mixture is smooth and creamy, adding more water if necessary.

Topping Ideas

When it comes to toppings, the sky's the limit. Consider classic combinations like bell peppers, onions, and mushrooms, or try out more unique options like artichoke hearts, olives, or even pineapple for a sweet twist. For protein, consider adding slices of plant-based sausage or tofu.

Baking Instructions

1. Preheat your oven to its highest temperature, usually around 500 degrees F (260 degrees C).
2. Punch down the dough and turn it out onto a floured surface. Roll out the dough into your desired thickness.
3. If you have a pizza stone, place it in the oven while preheating and transfer your rolled pizza dough onto the hot stone. Place your pizza dough on a baking sheet if you don't have a pizza stone.

4. Spread a thin layer of cashew cheese onto the pizza dough, leaving a small border for the crust.
5. Arrange your chosen toppings over the cashew cheese.
6. Bake the pizza in your oven for 10-15 minutes or until the crust is golden and the cashew cheese is slightly bubbly.

<u>Serving Suggestions</u>

Once your pizza is baked to perfection, please remove it from the oven and let it cool for a few minutes before slicing. This allows the cashew cheese to set a bit and makes slicing easier. Garnish with fresh basil leaves for a pop of color and freshness. Slice the pizza using a pizza cutter or a large sharp knife.

And there you have it, a plant-based pizza that will satisfy your cravings. Each bite offers a medley of textures and flavors - the crust's crunch, the cashew cheese's creaminess, and the toppings' freshness. This pizza is a testament to the versatility of plant-based ingredients, showcasing how they can be transformed into a dish that's both comforting and nourishing. So, whether you're hosting a pizza party or enjoying a quiet night, this plant-based pizza will surely be a hit. Enjoy the process of making it, the anticipation of baking it, and the satisfaction of savoring it. Here's to the joy of plant-based eating, one slice at a time.

### 12.2 VEGAN SHEPHERD'S PIE

*(Serves 4-6 people, 250-350 cal/serving, medium bowl. Green*

*lentils are an excellent source of plant-based protein and fiber. They provide essential nutrients like iron and folate).*

Picture a comforting dish brimming with a savory medley of vegetables and lentils, topped with a creamy layer of mashed potatoes, and baked to golden perfection. Yes, we're talking about Shepherd's Pie, a classic dish that's about to get a plant-based makeover. Let's roll up our sleeves and create a Vegan Shepherd's Pie that's as nourishing as it is delicious.

<u>Vegetable Filling Recipe</u>

The heart of our Shepherd's Pie is the hearty vegetable filling. This filling is a colorful array of vegetables and lentils, all simmered in a savory sauce.

<u>Ingredients</u>:

- 1 cup green lentils
- 2 carrots, peeled and diced
- 2 celery stalks, diced
- 1 onion, diced
- 2 cloves of garlic, minced
- 1 cup frozen peas
- 1 cup vegetable broth
- 2 tablespoons tomato paste
- 1 teaspoon thyme
- 1 teaspoon rosemary
- Salt and pepper to taste
- 1 tablespoon olive oil

Instructions:

1. Heat the olive oil in a large skillet over medium heat. Add the diced onion, carrots, and celery, cooking until the vegetables soften and the onion becomes translucent.
2. Stir in the minced garlic, thyme, and rosemary, cooking for another minute until the herbs are fragrant.
3. Add the green lentils, frozen peas, vegetable broth, and tomato paste to the skillet. Stir everything together until the tomato paste is well incorporated.
4. Bring the mixture to a simmer and cook for about 25 minutes, or until the lentils are tender and the

liquid is mostly absorbed—season with salt and pepper to taste.

Mashed Potato Topping Recipe

Next, we'll prepare the mashed potato topping. This creamy, fluffy layer is the crowning glory of our Shepherd's Pie, adding a comforting touch to the dish.

Ingredients:

- 4 large potatoes, peeled and cut into chunks
- 1/4 cup unsweetened almond milk
- 2 tablespoons vegan butter
- Salt and pepper to taste

Instructions:

1. Place the potato chunks in a large pot and cover with water. Bring the pot to a boil and let the potatoes cook until they're tender about 15 minutes.
2. Drain the potatoes and return them to the pot. Add the almond milk and vegan butter, seasoning with salt and pepper.
3. Mash the potatoes until they're creamy and smooth. If you prefer a chunkier texture, mash them less.

Baking Instructions

With our filling and topping ready, it's time to assemble and bake our Vegan Shepherd's Pie.

1. Preheat your oven to 400°F (200°C) and lightly grease a baking dish.
2. Spread the vegetable and lentil filling evenly in the baking dish.
3. Spoon the mashed potatoes over the filling, spreading them out to cover it completely.
4. Use a fork to create ridges in the mashed potatoes. These ridges will brown beautifully in the oven, adding a delightful crunch.
5. Bake the Shepherd's Pie in the preheated oven for about 25-30 minutes, until the mashed potatoes are golden brown and the edges are bubbling.

Serving and Storage Tips

Allow your Vegan Shepherd's Pie to rest briefly before serving. This allows the filling to set a bit and makes serving easier. To serve, scoop a generous portion onto a plate and enjoy it while it's warm—the savory filling, creamy mashed potatoes, and crispy top delight every bite.

If you have leftovers, they can be stored in the refrigerator in an airtight container for up to 3 days. To reheat, place in a preheated oven until warmed through. You can also freeze individual portions for a quick and comforting meal any day of the week.

So, there you have it, a Vegan Shepherd's Pie that's sure to warm your heart and nourish your body. Each forkful brings together the hearty filling and creamy topping, creating a harmony of flavors and textures that's genuinely satisfying. From the humble lentils to the comforting potatoes, each ingredient contributes its unique nutritional profile to this dish, creating a balanced meal that's as delicious as it is nutritious. So, enjoy the process of making it, the comforting aroma that fills your kitchen as it bakes, and the satisfaction of knowing you're creating a dish that's as good for your body as it is for your soul. Here's to comfort food, plant-based style!

### 12.3 Vegan Mac and Cheese

*(Serves 4-6 people, 150-200 cal/serving, one medium bowl. Cashews provide healthy fats, protein, and essential minerals like magnesium and phosphorus. They contribute to the creamy texture of the dish).*

### Pasta Selection

Choosing the right pasta is the starting point of your vegan mac and cheese adventure. Elbow macaroni is the classic choice for this dish, with its tubular shape that's perfect for holding creamy sauce. However, use other short pasta shapes like shells, fusilli, or rigatoni. Opt for whole wheat pasta for a boost in fiber and nutrients or gluten-free pasta if you're catering to dietary restrictions.

### Vegan Cheese Sauce Recipe

Next, let's create our velvety vegan cheese sauce. This dairy-free wonder gets its creamy texture from cashews and its rich, cheesy flavor from nutritional yeast.

Ingredients:

- 1 cup of raw cashews, soaked overnight
- 2 cups of water
- 1/4 cup of nutritional yeast
- 1/2 teaspoon of turmeric
- 1 teaspoon of paprika
- Salt to taste

Instructions:

1. Drain and rinse the soaked cashews, then add them to a blender with the water, nutritional yeast, turmeric, paprika, and salt.
2. Blend until the mixture is smooth and creamy, adding more water if necessary.

### Optional Add-Ins

Feel free to customize your vegan mac and cheese with additional flavors or ingredients. Stir in some cayenne pepper or hot sauce for a hint of heat. Fresh herbs like chives or parsley can add color and freshness. Plant-based sausage or smoky tempeh bacon can be a delicious addition if you crave something meaty.

### Baking Instructions

With our pasta cooked and our cheese sauce ready, it's time to assemble and bake our vegan mac and cheese.

1. Preheat your oven to 350°F (175°C) and lightly grease a baking dish.
2. Combine the cooked pasta and cheese sauce in a large bowl, stirring to ensure every piece of pasta is coated in the creamy sauce.
3. Transfer the mixture to your prepared baking dish, spreading it out evenly.
4. Bake in the oven for about 20 minutes or until the top is golden and the sauce bubbles.

### Serving Suggestions

Once your vegan mac and cheese is golden and bubbly, please remove it from the oven and let it cool for a few minutes. This allows the sauce to thicken slightly and makes serving easier. To serve, spoon a generous helping onto a plate and enjoy it while it's warm. A side of steamed broccoli or a fresh green salad can balance out the richness of the mac and cheese, creating a well-rounded meal. So go ahead and dig into this comfort classic that's as good for your body as it is for your soul.

### 12.4 Vegan Chocolate Chip Cookies

*(Makes around 24 cookies, 100-150 cal/cookie. Vegan butter is a dairy-free alternative that reduces saturated fat and cholesterol compared to traditional butter).*

Ingredients:

- 2 cups of your chosen flour
- 1 teaspoon baking soda
- 1/2 teaspoon salt.
- 1 cup of vegan butter
- 1 cup of brown sugar
- 1/2 cup of white sugar,

- 1 teaspoon of vanilla extract
- 2 tablespoons of unsweetened applesauce
- 1 1/2 cups of vegan chocolate chips.

There's something incredibly comforting about a chocolate chip cookie. Its warmth, sweetness, and delightful crumble are a treat that brings joy to any moment. Let's recreate this beloved classic in a vegan, plant-based style.

Flour Options

Choosing the suitable flour sets the foundation for your vegan chocolate chip cookies. All-purpose flour is the standard go-to, providing a reliable structure and texture. If you're looking for a whole grain option, whole wheat flour can offer a nuttier flavor and additional fiber. For those with gluten sensitivities, a gluten-free all-purpose flour blend can be used as a direct substitute.

Vegan Chocolate Chip Choices

Chocolate chips bring that sweetness and richness that's iconic in a chocolate chip cookie. When selecting chocolate chips for vegan cookies, read the ingredients, as some brands include milk products. Several brands offer vegan chocolate chips with cocoa, sugar, and plant-based stabilizers.

Baking Instructions

Your chosen flour and vegan chocolate chips are about to unite in cookie harmony. Start by preheating your oven to 350°F (175°C) and lining a baking sheet with parchment paper. Whisk together 2 cups of your chosen flour, one teaspoon of baking soda, and 1/2 teaspoon salt in a bowl. In a separate bowl, combine 1 cup of vegan butter, 1 cup of brown sugar, and 1/2 cup of white sugar, beating until creamy. Stir in 1 teaspoon of vanilla extract and two tablespoons of unsweetened applesauce, which acts as an egg substitute. Gradually mix the dry ingredients until combined, then fold in 1 1/2 cups of vegan chocolate chips.

Drop rounded tablespoons of dough onto your prepared baking sheet, spacing them about 2 inches apart. Bake for 10-12 minutes, or until golden brown.

<u>Cooling and Storage Tips</u>

Once your vegan chocolate chip cookies are perfectly baked, remove them from the oven. Let them cool on the baking sheet for about 5 minutes—this allows them to firm up a bit and makes them easier to transfer. Move the cookies to a wire rack to cool completely.

An airtight container is your best friend when storing your vegan chocolate chip cookies. Stored at room temperature, your cookies will stay fresh for about a week. If you want to extend their shelf life, you can freeze them in a freezer-safe container for up to 3 months. Just let them thaw at room temperature when ready to enjoy them.

And there you have it—a warm, sweet, and utterly delightful vegan chocolate chip cookie. It's proof that plant-based eating can be just as sweet, comforting, and delicious. So go ahead, take a bite. Let the cookie crumble, the chocolate melt, and the sweetness spread. This is more than just a cookie—it's a moment of joy, a slice of comfort, a taste of the sweet life of plant-based eating.

As we wrap up this chapter, let's take a moment to appreciate the delicious diversity of plant-based cuisine. From pizzas to shepherd's pies and mac and cheese to chocolate chip cookies, we've discovered that any dish can be recreated in a plant-based style. In doing so, we've nourished our bodies with wholesome ingredients and savored plant-based cooking flavors, textures, and joys. So, as we move forward in our culinary adventure, let's continue to explore, experiment, and enjoy the boundless possibilities of plant-based cuisine.

**You Have the Power to Inspire Change!**

You have an exciting future of culinary adventures and good health to look forward to–and what better time to inspire someone else to make the change?

Simply by sharing your honest opinion of this book and a little about your own journey into plant-based eating, you'll show new readers where they can find all the guidance they need to make this change themselves.

Thank you so much for your support. It's more powerful than you realize.

## THE BEGINNERS PLANT-POWERED DIET GUIDE & COOKBOOK

# EPILOGUE

Reflecting on Your Plant-Based Journey

As we turn the last page of this book, let's take a moment to reflect on the journey you've embarked upon. Embracing a plant-based lifestyle is not merely about changing your diet—it's about transforming your perspective on nourishing your body, respecting the environment, and making compassionate choices. It's not about perfection but striving for progress, one meal at a time.

Overcoming Potential Obstacles

Throughout this journey, you may face challenges or obstacles. You may find it difficult to resist the allure of old eating habits or to navigate social situations where plant-based options are scarce. Remember, it's okay to stumble. What's important is that you rise each time, armed with the knowledge that every choice you make brings you a step closer to wellness, compassion, and sustainability.

. . .

## Celebrating Small Victories

In this journey, no victory is too small to celebrate. Did you successfully make a plant-based version of your favorite childhood dish? Did you inspire a friend or family member to try a plant-based meal? Each of these moments is a testament to your commitment and the positive impact of your choices. So, relish these victories, for they fuel your journey and inspire those around you.

### Planning for a Sustainable Future

As you move forward, consider how to make this lifestyle sustainable. This might mean planning meals, growing vegetables, or exploring local farmers' markets. Remember, a plant-based lifestyle is not a rigid regimen—it's a flexible, evolving journey that should adapt to your needs, preferences, and lifestyle.

### Final Thoughts and Next Steps

As we close this chapter, remember that the journey doesn't end here. You now possess the knowledge, skills, and inspiration to continue exploring the world of plant-based cuisine. Use the tools and lessons you've learned from this book to carve your unique path.

### Continuing Education and Exploration

The world of plant-based eating is vast and ever-evolving. Stay curious, continue to educate yourself, and remain open to new foods, flavors, and ideas. Embrace the joy of discovery, and remember each meal is an opportunity to nourish your body, respect our planet, and celebrate life.

Looking back, I remember transitioning to a plant-based diet early. I recall the challenges, the victories, and the transformative moments. Today, I relish the opportunity to guide others through this journey. So, as you close this book, remember that you're not alone in this journey. I'm here, cheering you on every step of the way.

Here's to the joy of plant-based eating, your health, and a sustainable and compassionate world. Here's to the amazing journey ahead.

# REFERENCES

- *Nutritional Update for Physicians: Plant-Based Diets - PMC* https://www.ncbi.nlm.nih.gov/pmc/articles/PMC3662288/
- *Plant-Based vs. Vegan Diet — What's the Difference?* https://www.healthline.com/nutrition/plant-based-diet-vs-vegan
- *Nutritional Update for Physicians: Plant-Based Diets - PMC* https://www.ncbi.nlm.nih.gov/pmc/articles/PMC3662288/
- *Plant-Based Dietary Patterns for Human and Planetary ...* https://www.ncbi.nlm.nih.gov/pmc/articles/PMC9024616/
- *The 18 Best Protein Sources for Vegans and Vegetarians* https://www.healthline.com/nutrition/protein-for-vegans-vegetarians
- *Vitamin B12 deficiency can be sneaky and harmful* https://www.health.harvard.edu/blog/vitamin-

# REFERENCES

b12-deficiency-can-be-sneaky-harmful-201301105780

- *How to Understand and Use the Nutrition Facts Label* https://www.fda.gov/food/nutrition-facts-label/how-understand-and-use-nutrition-facts-label
- *Benefits and Risks of Taking Dietary Supplements* https://www.verywellfit.com/benefits-and-risks-of-taking-dietary-supplements-2506547
- *12 Must-Have Kitchen Tools for Plant-Based Cooking* https://www.plantbasedcooking.com/12-must-have-kitchen-tools-for-plant-based-cooking/
- *10 Essential Plant-based Pantry Staples* https://www.veganrunnereats.com/216/vegan-pantry-10-essential-foods-that-make-your-plant-based-diet-nutritious-and-healthy/
- *The Official 15 Most Vegan-Friendly Supermarkets In America* https://www.livekindly.com/official-15-vegan-friendly-supermarkets-america/
- *Fresh is Best; Vegan Food Storage to Prevent Waste* https://www.dephna.com/insights/vegan-food-storage-to-prevent-food-waste
- *10 Essential Plant-Based Cooking Tips* https://sharonpalmer.com/10-essential-plant-based-cooking-tips/
- *A Beginner's Guide to Vegan Meal Prep* https://www.thefullhelping.com/a-beginners-guide-to-vegan-meal-prep/

# REFERENCES

- *Grain and Legume Cooking Time Chart* http://www.veganbaking.net/articles/tools/grain-and-legume-cooking-chart
- *11 Tips for Making Tastier Plant-Based Meals, According ...* https://www.realsimple.com/food-recipes/cooking-tips-techniques/tastier-plant-based-meals
- *Light-as-a-Feather Whole Wheat Pancakes* https://www.centerfornutritionandathletics.org/recipees/light-as-a-feather-whole-wheat-pancakes/
- *The Ultimate Vegan Breakfast Tacos* https://www.feastingathome.com/the-ultimate-vegan-breakfast-tacos/
- *7 Enticing Health Benefits of Chia Seeds* https://www.healthline.com/nutrition/11-proven-health-benefits-of-chia-seeds
- *Green Smoothie Bowls 3 Ways (Vegan)* https://www.crowdedkitchen.com/green-smoothie-bowls-3-ways/
- *Quinoa: Nutrition Facts and Health Benefits* https://www.healthline.com/nutrition/8-health-benefits-quinoa
- *Recipe: Spicy Lentil Wraps with Tahini Sauce* https://www.thekitchn.com/recipe-spicy-lentil-wrap-with-tahini-saucerecipes-from-the-kitchn-167629
- *Hearty Minestrone Soup Recipe* https://www.tastingtable.com/1041869/hearty-minestrone-soup-recipe/

## REFERENCES

- *Easy Homemade Vegan Sushi Recipe* https://www.veggiesdontbite.com/homemade-vegan-sushi-recipes/
- *31 Easy Plant-Based Recipes* https://www.loveandlemons.com/plant-based-recipes/
- *What is a plant-based diet, and why should you try it?* https://www.health.harvard.edu/blog/what-is-a-plant-based-diet-and-why-should-you-try-it-2018092614760
- *20 Vegan Cooking Tips For Beginners* https://ohmyveggies.com/vegan-cooking-tips-for-beginners/
- *Plant-Based Diets* https://www.pcrm.org/good-nutrition/plant-based-diets
- *Is Hummus Healthy? Top 8 Benefits of Hummus* https://www.healthline.com/nutrition/is-hummus-healthy
- *Roasted Brussels Sprouts with Balsamic Vinegar & Honey* https://www.onceuponachef.com/recipes/roasted-brussels-sprouts.html
- *Healthy Sweet Potato Fries with Avocado Dip* https://www.delscookingtwist.com/healthy-sweet-potato-fries-with-avocado-dip/
- *Healthy Baked Falafel Recipe* https://joyfoodsunshine.com/baked-falafel/
- *Authentic Thai Green Curry Recipe (แกงเขียวหวาน) by My ...* https://www.eatingthaifood.com/thai-green-curry-recipe/

# REFERENCES

- *Mexican Black Beans for Tacos - Quick and Easy* https://bitesofwellness.com/mexican-black-beans-for-tacos/
- *Best Vegan Lasagna Recipe (with Béchamel)* https://simplyceecee.co/vegan-lasagna-with-bechamel/
- *Veg Biryani Recipe (Hyderabadi Vegetable Dum Biryani)* https://www.vegrecipesofindia.com/hyderabad-veg-biryani-hyderabadi-vegetable-dum-biryani-recipe/
- *Are Plant-Based Desserts Better For You?* https://simplydelish.net/sd-blog/plant-based-desserts-are-good-for-you/
- *The Ultimate Guide to Vegan Baking Substitutes - livekindly* https://www.livekindly.com/guide-vegan-baking-substitutes/
- *Avocados | The Nutrition Source | Harvard T.H. Chan School ...* https://www.hsph.harvard.edu/nutritionsource/avocados/
- *30 Best Vegan Desserts* https://www.loveandlemons.com/vegan-desserts/
- *Green Smoothies: Are They Good for You? - WebMD* https://www.webmd.com/diet/green-smoothies-are-they-good-for-you
- *Healthy Hot Cocoa with Almond Milk (Vegan, Dairy-Free)* https://www.happyfoodstube.com/healthy-almond-milk-hot-cocoa-recipe/
- *Top 5 Benefits of a Healthy Berry Smoothie* https://smoothiebox.com/blogs/blog/top-5-benefits-of-a-healthy-berry-smoothie

## REFERENCES

- *Healthy Homemade Pumpkin Spice Latte* https://www.eatingbirdfood.com/healthy-homemade-pumpkin-spice-latte/
- *Homemade Oil-Free Vegan Pizza Dough* https://www.forksoverknives.com/recipes/vegan-baked-stuffed/oil-free-vegan-pizza-dough/
- *Go-to Cashew Cheese Recipe* https://www.thefullhelping.com/go-to-cashew-cheese-recipe/
- *26 Vegan Classics You Should Learn How To Cook* https://www.buzzfeed.com/michelleno/classic-beginner-vegan-recipes
- *The Ultimate Guide to Vegan Baking Substitutes - livekindly* https://www.livekindly.com/guide-vegan-baking-substitutes/
- Buxton, Amy. "42% Of Global Consumers Believe Plant-Based Food Will Replace Meat Within A Decade." Plant Based News. Last modified December 2, 2022. https://plantbasednews.org/news/environment/vegan-vegetarian-food-replace-meat-decade/.
- Jones, Luke. "50 Vegan Quotes from Plant-Based Pioneers" HERO Movement. Last modified January 16, 2015. https://www.heromovement.net/blog/vegan-quotes/.

Printed in Great Britain
by Amazon